THE ISLE OF WIGHT
COASTAL PATH

GW00392551

ALAN CHARLES

*Please respect the Country Code and help
keep the Island tidy.*

Royalties from the sale of this book are being donated to the
Third World development and relief agency, Christian Aid

Published by
THORNHILL PRESS
24 Moorend Road
Cheltenham
Glos.
MCMLXXXVI

ISBN 0 946328 13 7

Printed by
Stoate and Bishop (Printers) Ltd.,
Gloucester and Cheltenham

THE ISLE OF WIGHT COASTAL PATH

by ALAN CHARLES

Foreword: Professor David Bellamy

Cover drawings by Jenny Cooper, B.A.
formerly Warden of Whitwell Youth Hostel, Isle of Wight.

Other drawings by Leonard J. Hayes, R.I.B.A.

Maps drawn by the Author.

By the same author:
THE RIDGEWAY PATH
Spurbooks (Penguin)

FOREWORD

by PROFESSOR DAVID BELLAMY

The Needles, Alum and Freshwater Bay, Blackgang Chine, Cowes, all names which ring with childhood memories of happy days beside the sea — and many more to come.

The Isle of Wight has so much to offer in terms of holiday and heritage. Geology, history, literature, gardens, seafaring, smugglers, flora, fauna, messing about in boats, you name it, the Island's got it, somewhere.

The only problem is where to begin, for with such diversity at hand it is difficult to know just where to start and stop.

This guide changes all that: in practical terms it tells the would-be walkers how to discover it all for themselves.

Here is a guide that catches your imagination, grabs you by the feet and leads you ever on into heritage pastures new. There's no excuse now; you will have to return to the Isle of Wight again and again and again. It doesn't matter whether you are a fit long-distance walker or a family with toddlers and/or dodderers, the relevant information is here.

Bedburn

INTRODUCTION

If a mere mention of England's Garden Isle conjures up visions of crowded beaches, 'quaint' touristy villages, gaudy shops and fun parlours, then my first duty is to dispense reassurance. In the height of the summer season the Island's holiday population can indeed be quite dense, especially at Ventnor, Shanklin and Sandown; but the walker who enjoys his own or chosen company will find ample fulfilment along much of the Island's Coastal Path. And if the long days of May or June are chosen for a visit to the Island he will find that even the popular tourist centres are noticeably depopulated. That's bad for business, but good for solitude!

Having paid good money (I trust!) for this small volume you should know at the outset what you have let yourself in for! In theory approximately 67 miles of coast path lie before you; in practice the route is somewhat more diverse, with thirty-eight miles of paths that do indeed closely follow the coast; twelve miles of inland paths with little or no view of the sea or coast; eleven miles of quiet — mostly country-roads; and six miles of not-so-quiet roads.

I have divided the route into ten walks, each of which can be completed in the space of half-a-day or so. At this rate of progress a two-week holiday would allow time to complete the entire Island circuit in quite a leisurely fashion. The moderately energetic walker could complete the Path in about one week, but this would require careful planning in terms of accommodation and transport.

An essential item of equipment for the coast-path walker is a copy of the Southern Vectis timetable, which gives details of the excellent Island-wide bus service. If you arrive at the start of a walk by car you can be reasonably assured of catching a bus back to your vehicle after the walk is over. To help you in this I have entered the appropriate route numbers at the end of each chapter. This information is only meant to be a rough guide to available services (which can vary from year to year) so do please make sure that you carry an up-to-date copy of the time-table! These are available from many Island shops.

Another valuable investment is the Ordnance Survey Leisure Map No. 29. This is on a scale of 2½ ins. to the mile (4 cm. to 1 km.) and is overlaid with the Island's network of Public Rights of Way — including the Coastal Path. Useful information such as car parks, viewpoints, picnic sites etc. is also given.

The Island's coastline is under constant review by the forces of Nature, so that in many places you may find that the Path terminates abruptly. At such times a measure of initiative (or daring!) may be required if you are to make progress. The importance of well-shod feet in such circumstances cannot be over-emphasised. Heavy boots with layer upon layer of thick woollen socks may not be your style, but a pair of stout shoes with good welts and thick uppers should be the subject of serious consideration.

Accommodation

Some accommodation addresses are given at the end of each walk (these should be checked as they may alter).

The Isle of Wight Tourist Board publishes an annual holiday guide which includes in its pages a large number of accommodation addresses. Most of the entries are from the main tourist centres of Cowes, Ryde, Shanklin etc. with only a few from quiet coastal areas. However, the volume is cheap and contains a wealth of useful information. It is available from the Tourist Information Centre at 21, High Street, Newport, and from Mainland bookshops. The Ramblers & Cyclists Bed & Breakfast Guide is also available from bookshops (and direct from the Ramblers Association at 1/5 Wandsworth Road, London, SW8 2XX). This useful volume covers the whole of Britain and invariably includes a handful of recommended addresses for the Isle of Wight. From personal experience I can strongly recommend the Island's three permanent Youth Hostels: Totland, Whitwell and Sandown. They are convenient, comfortable and sociable. The temporary hostel at the Wootton Youth Centre is generally open from mid-July until the end of August and is suitable for those who are prepared to 'rough-it'. Camp beds in close formation in a large hall, and the absence of cooking facilities may not be to your liking. The YHA Handbook gives details of hostels and membership and can be purchased from bookshops or direct from Trevelyan House, St. Stephens Hill, St Albans, Herts. AL1 2DY. And don't be put off by the word 'Youth'; the only age limit is at the low end — five! (and even under 5's can be accommodated at some mainland hostels)

Land and Life

The Isle of Wight is often thought of as a 'microcosm of·England' in that the complexity and variety of Mainland landscape and wildlife is echoed across the Island, but on a smaller scale. It follows that a brief commentary on these subjects — one that fits the size of this book — may turn out to be inadequate or superficial. That's the risk I am about to take!

The most noticeable feature of the Island's geology is the massive belt of chalk that stretches from Whitecliff Bay and Culver in the east to The Needles in the west. Something of the depth of this chalk is revealed in vast white cliffs at these extremities of the Island. Outliers in the south have given rise to the Island's three highest points — St. Catherine's Down above Blackgang (236m), St. Boniface Down above Ventnor (235m), and Shanklin Down (235m). Much deeper than these southern formations lies a bed of sandrock. The attractive coastal region known as the Undercliff owes its existance, in the main, to this substance. Under its influence the land has slumped seaward to form a rugged landscape intermediate between upper and lower cliffs. The most highly acclaimed part of this region is the Landslip, east of Ventnor. This is a paradise of the natural world and is, in the words of Edward Thomas, 'a tumult of twisted oaks among rocks all upheaved and broken into caves and hillocks'. Elsewhere along the Island's coastline the clays and sands form relatively low-lying cliffs. Erosion of these cliffs is usually gradual but continuous, and often unnoticed except by those most directly concerned: farmers, local residents, highway engineers.

The diversity of the Island's geology and landscape leads to an equal diversity in wildlife. While the keen walker-cum-naturalist might absorb himself in the whole spectrum of plants and animals, I will confine my few comments to the two most commonly enjoyed subdivisions of the natural world — flowers and birds.

To equip yourself at the outset with, say, the pocket edition of the Oxford Book of Wild Flowers is to start off on the right foot. Together with an observant eye, it will lead you into a delightful botanical world to which fields and downland, woods and hedgerows, estuaries and the seashore, each make their special contribution. Even the unobservant may well be caught in his steps by some outstanding displays of colour or beauty; noteable examples being the acres of sea lavender alongside Newtown Estuary or the carpets of sea pinks beside the cliff path of the south-west coast. Perhaps the most highly esteemed of our wild flowers are those that prefer — or are confined to — chalky soils. Among the many species that you are likely to see are self-heal and wild thyme; birdsfoot trefoil and kidney vetch; carline and dwarf thistles; scabious, rock-rose, and eyebright. Up on the heights of Culver Down, Highdown, and Tennyson Down these plants are in places reduced to stunted forms by the constraints of wind and weather.

Although there are many different habitats for birds on the Island the coastal region is the one that comes most readily to mind. With many of the birds well-and-truly keeping their distance the possession of a good pair of binoculars can substantially increase the pleasure and satisfaction in identifying species. A size '8 x 40' binocular is a good compromise between magnification and stability; and a wide field-of-view is a useful feature when attempting to 'capture' a bird. Add to this a copy of the 'Field Guide to the Birds of Britain and Europe' and you're made! Out of the formidable catalogue of birds of the coast come such names as cormorant, guillemot, razorbill, puffin, fulmer, kittiwake, oyster-catcher, ringed plover, dunlin and curlew; but if you are in too much of a hurry you may observe no more than cormorants, oyster-catchers and herring gulls!

Newtown Estuary on the north-west coast is the Island's Mecca for birds (and birdwatchers!). 168 species are known to inhabit the creeks, marshes and fields thereabouts. Included are such names as shelduck, wigeon, red-breasted merganser, teal, redshank, dunlin, and black-tailed godwit. And even such rarities as the avocet and osprey have made occasional appearances in the area.

Finally, to Man himself. Apart from roads, I think the most indelible mark of his presence exists in the form of the Island's coastal defences. With the important harbours of Southampton and Portsmouth sheltering behind its protective shield, the Island's strategic importance is beyond question. Henry VIII was well aware of this when he built castles at Yarmouth, Cowes and Sandown. Following Lord Palmerston's 1859 Royal Commission — which was set up to 'Consider the Defences of the United Kingdom' — new batteries were built and old ones modified and extended. This expensive exercise was designed to counteract the imagined threat of a French invasion, a threat that almost led to panic. As far as I know not one shot was fired in anger, at least not until the Second World War when these same batteries, modified yet again, were used in the defence of Britain.

Map Symbols

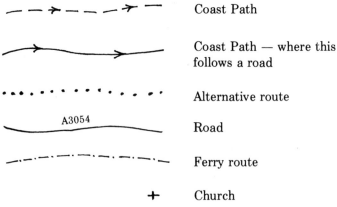

— — ⤚ — — — ⤚ —	Coast Path
⟶ ⟶ —	Coast Path — where this follows a road
• • • • • • • • • • • • •	Alternative route
A3054	Road
—·—·—·—·—·—·—·—	Ferry route
+	Church

ISLE OF WIGHT COASTAL FOOTPATH

1. YARMOUTH TO FRESHWATER BAY

DISTANCES: Alum Bay 5 miles (8km); Freshwater Bay 9 miles (14.5km)

CAR PARKING at Yarmouth (1) River Road Car Park, beside the A3054

(2) Roadside parking at The Common (picnic area) east of the town

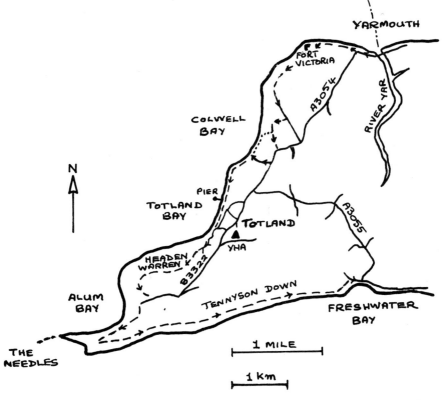

This coast of 'West Wight' has much to offer in variety of scene and historical interest, as well as in the sheer delight and exhilaration of walking. Highdown and Tennyson Down take pride of place with their breathtaking Island-wide views. Historically the coast is alive with interest, especially for those with an eye for Victorian military archaeology. Foremost in the mind will be Fort Victoria and the Old Needles Battery, because these have been preserved and are open to the public. Since your day may be too short to visit these two sites *and* walk all the way to Freshwater Bay you may decide to 'call a halt' at Alum Bay and return to Yarmouth by bus. Those who wish to *start* walking from Alum Bay should commence reading at **(1)** on page 15.

Youth Hostellers bound for Totland will find that Totland's pier or (much later) Tennyson Down are convenient points from which to leave the Coast Path. Directions for these 'spurs' are given in the text.

The best place from which to start the day's walk is at the entrance to Yarmouth's Victorian pier. The pier was opened in 1876 and until recent years was certainly showing its age. Following a public inquiry in 1982 the Yarmouth Harbour Commissioners were refused permission to demolish this 'grade II listed building'. It has now undergone an extensive (and expensive) programme of restoration.

If you stand with your back to the pier Yarmouth Castle will be on your right. This is one of a series of forts planned by Henry VIII in 1538 as a defensive measure against the French. It was designed specifically for the use of cannon, with a low platform but without the conventional tower. Henry's coat-of-arms can be seen above the original entrance gate in the east wall. The castle is open to the public. The George Hotel next door was owned by Admiral Sir Robert Holmes in the 1600's. He is remembered (perhaps erroniously) for giving New York its name, after its capture from the Dutch in 1664. The hotel includes a room used by King Charles II in 1671. Closer at hand on the wall bordering the castle precincts, are old posters, in stone, advertising early charabanc services.

By now you will be champing at the bit; so let's get started! Walk forward from the pier to the first turning on the right — Queen Street; but before making that turn note the old Town Hall directly ahead. This dates back to 1763 (or earlier) and remains in use right up to the present day. Going along Queen Street you will pass the entrance to Yarmouth Castle on your right. Turn left at the harbour and go past the lifeboat office. On the outside wall there is a detailed list of the 'assistance given' since 1957. You can expect to see the lifeboat close at hand in the harbour — if it is not out on some errand of mercy. Now go forward to join the main road (A3054); turn right into this and proceed to the new bridge over the River Yar. The earlier swing bridge started life as far back as 1863, and had well and truly served its time.

The first building on the right beyond the river is The Sandhouse. Sand from Alum Bay was once stored here before being shipped to the mainland for glassmaking. When the road turns sharp left go right into a track signposted 'Victoria Park/Sea Wall'. Passing public toilets immediately on the right walk down to the new sea wall. Turn left here and go along this new section of wall to its far end where a wood ends (more or less). Go left here, up a short flight of steps leading to a footpath and then to a road. Go forward in the road for 100 man-size paces (70 yards) to a drive on the left. Here you have the option of turning left into the drive or staying in the road for Fort Victoria, a short worthwhile diversion if you are interested in military archaeology or are in need of refreshment. You could have a look at the fort and meet the coast path a little further along. Admission is free (bless the thought!) as are the conducted tours which take place on Sundays and Wednesdays from mid-April onwards. If none of this appeals, then turn left into the drive. When the drive turns right to some houses continue straight on along a footpath. You will eventually meet a path coming up from the right — from the fort. You should now read on from **(2)** below.

Victoria is the third fort to be built here since 1547, and dates back to 1853. Together with its opposite number at Hurst Point on the mainland, Fort Victoria's purpose was to defend the Needles Passage against possible enemy incursion. However, it has performed a variety of military functions over the years. The reward for services rendered was the shameful demolition of a large part of its structure prior to purchase by the Isle of Wight County Council. Railway enthusiasts will find their pulse quickened when they discover a short section of 18-inch track outside the cafe. This is a relic of a light railway that was used to transport mines from the now disused pier (the one that you passed on your way down to the fort).

To rejoin the Coast Path go along the footpath that starts at the inland extremity of the fort. This path turns left beside a picnic area and enters the wood. Follow the path up to a T-junction, at which turn right.

(2) Go forward in the long straight woodland path. This eventually turns half-left, with steps leading uphill, bringing you out into the open and on to a ledge. I hope your weather is fine, so that you can enjoy the excellent view across Needles Passage, with Hurst Castle and two lighthouses out on a limb at the end of a long narrow spit. Like so many coastal forts, Hurst originated with Henry VIII, the circular keep dating from his time. In the nineteenth century the castle was extended to include no less than 61 casemates (gunports) — enough to scare the living daylights out of any would-be agressors. Ignore a short flight of steps on the left and go forward to join a tarmac path, with a wood on the right. The residue of Cliff End Battery can be seen beyond the wood. Completed in 1871 the battery was one of numerous coastal defences (including Hurst Castle mentioned above) proposed for England and Wales in a Royal Commission Report of 1859. The Commission was formed following anxiety over the mounting strength of the French Navy. Cliff End Battery remained in use until after the Second World War.

The path turns left here, then right, then left, then right again; then between fields to a stile at a road. Turn left at the road (or right for a good view of Cliff End Battery and Fort Albert) and follow this downhill. You should now see — weather permitting — the Needles rocks and their lighthouse 3 miles to the south-west. The road climbs to a junction, where you should turn right and walk down through a permanent holiday site. Here you will find 'Brambles Chine Club Bar' and two large cedar trees on the left. After passing the cedars and the next line of holiday houses, turn left into a concrete drive. This soon leads into a footpath running between hedges. The path turns right and eventually meets a track, with an iron gate on the left. Turn right here, into the lowest of two tracks. This will take you down to the beach at Brambles Chine. Since the coast path has disappeared from the clifftop at this point you have instead the prospect of a short walk along the beach to Colwell Chine. If the sea is too high for safety then I'm afraid it's an about turn along an inland route to Colwell. Directions for this detour (which you may well find signposted) are given at the end of this chapter.

Before making that choice you should look along the coast in the reverse direction for a view of Fort Albert. To avoid the risk of boring you with yet more military history I'll keep it short. Built in the 1850's Fort Albert's chief claim to fame seems to be that it functioned as an experimental station for an early type of torpedo, the Brennan. The design of the torpedo is interesting in that it was guided by wire run out from the shore. Going along the beach you will soon join the sea wall **(3)** leading to Colwell: a resort in miniature, with the usual complement of beach huts and ice-cream parlours. Stay with the sea wall all the way to the pier at Totland Bay.

The pier is a good point from which to break off for the Yarmouth bus or Totland Youth Hostel. To do this you should ascend the flight of steps directly opposite the pier; turn right at the top and proceed to a crossroad. Go along the road signposted to Totland (Madeira Road), passing Sentry Mead Hotel on the left. This will take you to Totland War Memorial and the bus stop (route 7/7A to Yarmouth). Hostellers should go into Weston Road (from the War Memorial) and follow this to its meeting with Hurst Hill and York Road. The hostel is on the left in Hurst Hill.

Now back to Totland's pier. Continuing along the sea wall you will soon notice a signpost pointing uphill to Totland's Turf Walk. This is a delightful piece of greensward at the top of the cliff, with a fine view and plenty of seats. If you opt for this short diversion you could rejoin the coast path by going west along the Turf Walk to its meeting with a road at the far end. Go forward in the road until you reach the first left-hand bend; then read on from **(4)** below.

The official route continues along the sea wall almost to its end — at the Old Lifeboat Station. At least six stations existed on the Island in earlier days. Now there are two (Inshore Stations apart); these are at Yarmouth and Bembridge where lifeboats are equipped with modern radio and navigational aids. Just beyond the 'station' a steep path takes you back uphill to a road.

(4) Go straight on up the road and when this bends left turn right into a path signposted to Alum Bay. This soon turns left and places you on National Trust land (Headon Warren) where a clear uphill path cuts through the undergrowth. You will meet a crossing of ways soon after coming out into the open, where you should continue straight on uphill. Ignore the first left-hand branch in the path (just beyond a seat on the right) and walk on up to the second. Fork left here and go up to the fence protecting a tumulus at the summit of the Warren. This is one of the Island's Bronze Age burial mounds — visible reminders of man's presence more than 2,700 years ago. These mounds are a source of anxiety to the archaeologist, being constantly under threat from ploughing, forestry, coastal erosion, rabbits, thoughtless treasure hunters and, as was the case here — tourists' feet.

Going westward along the summit ridge you will pass a seat on the left before crossing four man-hole covers (here of all places!) Ignore a downward path just here and continue on the level for a short distance to the next downward — but forward — path. This will take you down to a left-hand hairpin bend beside a National Trust donation plinth; an opportunity to empty your pockets and to contemplate the outstanding work of the Trust in preserving our coastal heritage! Pause also to examine the derelict Hatherwood Point Battery. This is another of those defence works originating from the 1859 Royal Commission. Frequent changes of mind over the most suitable armament resulted in the battery being repeatedly modified and extended over a space of 12 years. The site was finally abandoned in 1925.

As you go left with the hairpin bend you will be at the start of a long zig-zag path which eventually leads you down to a wooden gate. (Short-circuiting the zig-zag will hasten your descent but may well lead you astray; so be warned!) Continue straight on from the wooden gate and turn right into the road ahead. **(1)** Now brace yourself for the spectacle of Alum Bay — a striking contrast to the idyllic heights of Headon Warren! If you decide to run the gauntlet through all this to the Bay itself, your reward will be a close encounter with the renowned Alum Bay cliff and its spectrum of coloured sands.

Closer at hand in its undignified position at the centre of the car park a monument marks the site of Guglielmo Marconi's first coastal wireless station, which was set up in 1897. Marconi's exciting experiments — which "attracted world attention" — are described on the four faces of the monument.

Marconi Memorial

If you plan a visit to the Old Needles Battery you could join the National Trust minibus which takes you all the way, but to enjoy the prospect of Alum Bay to the full (with all but the chair lift well out of sight) you must walk! The Battery is well worth a visit (at such a modest admission price!) and offers the finest view of the Needles and its lighthouse that you could ever hope to get from dry land. It was opened to the public by the Prince of Wales in 1982, 99 years after its completion as a defence work.

Assuming you have decided against a lift on the National Trust minibus you should walk up the Needles Battery drive, passing the public toilets and a coach park on your left. Stay with the drive when it turns right just beyond some cottages. Less than ½ mile from this right hand turn a path goes off half-left up the hillside (National Trust indicator board 'West High Down'). Stay in the drive if you are heading for the Battery (see directions at the end of this chapter for rejoining the coast path after your visit); otherwise take this steep uphill path to a stile just below a terrace of National Trust holiday cottages (ex Coast Guard).

Your next move should normally be to go left in hairpin fashion (without crossing the stile) so that the cottages appear uphill on your right; but if you go over the stile, and follow the 'Needles Viewpoint' sign, you will see, in addition to the Needles, an abandoned rocket test site on the southern slope of the down. In the event of the 'Viewpoint' sign disappearing, the precise route from the stile is as follows: go uphill in the drive ahead and fork right into another drive almost immediately. This will take you alongside the *New* Needles Battery. Go left with this drive at the far end of the Battery: the Test Site is then directly ahead and The Needles Viewpoint beyond a chalky mound on the right. The Test Site was used by the renowned Saunders Roe Company from 1956 onwards for the testing of the Black Knight rocket which was to form part of the Blue Streak missile. The New Needles Battery was built in the early 1890's and it was there, in 1913, that the first British anti-aircraft gun (the 'Pom-Pom') was tested.

Now back to that stile and the hairpin turn mentioned earlier: **(5)** go uphill from the stile in an easterly direction, with the National Trust cottages on your right. This takes you up to the top of West High Down. From here you should see St. Catherine's Point — given good visibility and good eyesight — and its lighthouse at the southernmost extremity of the Island. What you shouldn't see are the sheer chalk cliffs which separate these downs from the sea! It is for the birds to enjoy sovereignty there, in more-or-less complete isolation from man. Continuing on now you will eventually come to a stand of hawthorns at a dip in the downs. There is a stile and a seat, and a half-size replica of a navigation beacon that once stood on Tennyson Down. The path divides just here. Take the right hand branch; this leads you uphill to Tennyson's Monument.

Alfred Lord Tennyson, the Victorian poet, came to Farringford House Freshwater in 1853, largely to escape publicity. This move was not entirely successful: he was often harried by sightseers — especially when taking his daily walk over High Down. He moved to Aldworth in Sussex in 1869 in a further flight from publicity, returning to the Island only during the winter and spring months.

At the end of this chapter you will find directions to take you from Tennyson's Monument to Totland — for the Youth Hostel or the Yarmouth bus.

It's a clear run down to Freshwater now: you will pass more hawthorns (on the left) and a seat (on the right), followed by a stile almost immediately. The final stretch is along a tarmac drive with a stone wall on the right. At the end of this turn right for Freshwater Bay and the refreshment houses.

Detour from Brambles Chine to Colwell

Engage reverse gear at Brambles Chine and go back along the path whence you came. When you reach that iron gate (at a corner), turn right and, after passing a farmhouse on the right, proceed to a road (A3054

Colwell Road). Turn right here and go along this to the first turning on the right, Madeira Lane. When Madeira Lane curves right beyond the houses go straight on down a path to the sea wall. Now back to **(3)** on page 14.

From Needles Old Battery back to the Coast Path

Very soon after leaving the Old Battery go half-right up a steep path; then round the left side of a wired enclosure containing a gantry. This will lead you almost immediately on to a drive that runs between the New Needles Battery and a disused rocket test site. Turning left in the drive and going ahead to a stile below a terrace of cottages will set you back on the coast path (continue from **(5)** on page 17). For a view of the Test Site and the Needles go right in the drive instead of left. For a description of the New Needles Battery and the Test Site see page 17.

From Tennyson Down to Totland and the Youth Hostel

From Tennyson's Monument walk inland in the direction of Hurst Castle on the mainland (if you can see it!) and down a narrow path through dense scrub. This path soon skirts the right hand edge of a chalk pit. After going round the lower edge of the pit turn right into a lane and follow this downhill.

Highdown Inn at the road junction ahead is notorious (historically!) for its smuggling associations. Cross the junction into Weston Lane and follow through to the junction with Hurst Hill. St. Saviour's Church is on the right and the 'superior' grade Youth Hostel directly ahead. Turn left into Hurst Hill then first right into Weston Road. This will take you down to Totland War Memorial, a good restaurant, and the Yarmouth bus.

Returning to Yarmouth

From Freshwater Bay: Bus 7, 7A or 46 (46 summer only).
From Alum Bay: Bus 42 direct to Yarmouth or 27, 28, 29 to Totland (All summer only) followed by 7 or 7A to Yarmouth.

Accommodation

Cambridge Lodge, Gate Lane, Freshwater. Tel. (0983) 753823.
The Corner House, Gate Lane, Freshwater. Tel. (0983) 753246.
Sandy Lane Guest House, Colwell Bay. Tel. (0983) 75333.
Youth Hostel, Hurst Hill, Totland Bay. Tel: (0983) 752165 (closed Sunday except during July and August).
For accommodation in Yarmouth see page 76.

Refreshments available at Yarmouth, Fort Victoria, Colwell Bay, Totland (The Broadway), Totland Pier, Alum Bay, Freshwater Bay.

2. FRESHWATER BAY TO GRANGE

DISTANCE: 6 miles (9.7km)

CAR PARKING at Freshwater (1) At the junction of Afton New Road and Military Road, directly opposite the Bay

(2) National Trust car park on Afton Down, ¼ mile east of the Bay

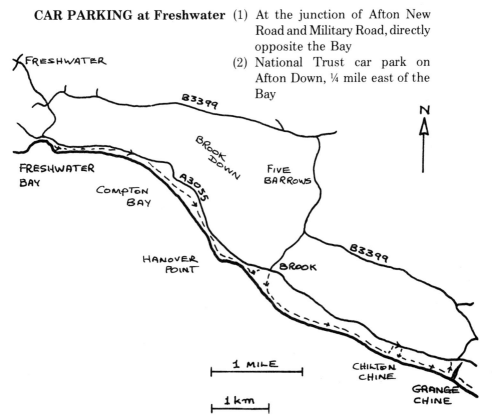

But for the initial steep rise and fall in the land east of Freshwater the uniformity of the south-west coast comes as a striking contrast to all that we have seen so far. The flat arable fields terminate more-or-less abruptly along a relatively low cliff edge, a cliff that gradually increases in height as it approaches Blackgang. The principal points of relief along this 12 mile length of coast are at the chines — fissures carved out of the cliff by water draining seaward from the fields. Although today's walk terminates about half way along this south-west coast, you may well be agile enough to complete the entire 12 miles to Blackgang in one go. In any case it is a simple matter to match distance to stamina by breaking away from the coast path along one of the many rights-of-way. These invariably run inland to meet the Military Road, which lies parallel to the

19

coast and carries the bus service to Freshwater and beyond.

Freshwater itself is worth a little of your time before you make a bee-line for the coast path. Farringford House, home of the nineteenth-century poet Alfred Lord Tennyson, can be viewed from Bedbury Lane (see page 17). The attractive thatched church of St. Agnes stands midway between Farringford and Freshwater Bay — in Gate Lane. The '1694' date stone may mislead you into thinking that the church is more than 200 years old. It was in fact built in 1908 from stone (including the date stone) salvaged from a derelict farmhouse. All Saints Church is equally attractive but lies further afield — at Hooke Hill beside the River Yar. Tennyson's wife Emily, his son Hallam and his grandson Lionel (the England cricketer) are buried there.

If you are starting from the National Trust car park on Afton Down you should cross the road and take your cue from **(6)** below. Otherwise, from Freshwater Bay, ascend the steps at the eastern end of the sea wall near the Inshore Rescue Station. This will lead you on to the cliff-top path (with a wire fence left) and then slightly inland to join the road **(6)** — at a bend. This is a good point from which to stand and stare. Looking back to the far side of Freshwater Bay you can see something of Freshwater Redoubt, a defence battery built in 1800. It is isolated on the landward side by a deep ditch, a clear feature from this angle. The large white building to the right of the Redoubt is a Holiday Fellowship guest house, an excellent establishment with three commendable objectives: good walking, good eating and good sociability. Further right still, on the horizon, is Tennyson's home, Farringford, standing behind a large blue cedar. And now with a 90 degree turn inland you have Afton Down and its golf course on an important archaeological site. A Neolithic (New Stone Age) long barrow 120 feet in length is situated south of the clubhouse, but this is only faintly visible from your present position. Numerous Bronze Age barrows are in view but it is difficult for lesser mortals (like myself) to distinguish these from the plethora of golfing bunkers. This 'cemetery' was identified in 1899 when 40 urns containing cremated remains were unearthed.

The path veers away from the road to a small memorial stone. This is inscribed with the sad tale of a 15 year old boy who fell from the cliff in 1846. A series of orange waymarks eventually takes us back to the A3055 — the Military Road. This road was built in the mid nineteenth-century for the rapid movement of troops and could not be used by the public until 1933. Between Freshwater and Brook the road is under constant threat from erosion and subsidence and sensitive monitoring equipment has been installed to give instant warning of any hazardous earth movement.

Just before a small National Trust car park (on the left of the road) a coastal path signpost on the right directs you down to the cliff edge. Once there you should follow the cliff edge downhill to a narrow ravine — the 'upper reach' of Compton Chine. Here begins dinosaur country. Along the seven coastal miles between Compton Chine and Atherfield Point, an outcrop of Wealden Marl — a sedimentary clayey material — has revealed fossilised bones of dinosaurs which walked these parts more than 100 million years ago. To those interested in the subject I would commend Mr. W. T. Blow's 'Reptiles on the Rocks'. This little book includes a very readable introduction to dinosaurs as well as an account of the author's discoveries on the Island.

After crossing the chine (there is a 'wreck post' just here — see page 43) turn half-left towards a memorial stone — inscribed to a World War II soldier — and a cottage beside the Military Road. Don't go into the road but turn right just before it and go up to a sunken path leading to a stile, passing a National Trust collecting box on the right. Beyond the stile you should work your way uphill to join a wire fence on the left. Thereafter the path meanders for ¾ mile between the wire fence and the upper cliff edge. Just before Shippards Chine turn left to a stile in the far corner of a field; then rejoin the cliff path by crossing the National Trust car park. The stone plinth set in the sea bed marks Hanover Point, and was used by gunners at Freshwater Redoubt to set their landward limit during practice firings. The beach around Hanover Point is famous among geologists for its beds of fossilised pine wood, exposed only at low tide. Much of this wood has unfortunately disappeared due to wave action and the enthusiasm of rockery builders.

Looking inland you now have sight of Brook Hill House about one mile eastward. This was for some years the home of playwright and novelist J. B. Priestley, and has now been divided into luxury flats. In June the blue haze of rhododendrons in the grounds of the House can be seen from the coast. Continuing on now you will go over a stile and an improvised footbridge; and at the next stile you will be overlooking Brook Chine. Take my advice and don't attempt a direct crossing of the chine from this point. I have it on good authority that the village septic tank often overflows into it. So, go over the stile, turn left, and rejoin the Military Road. Turn right in the road and go ahead to the Brook turn-off. Brook is an attractive, unspoilt village with a history closely woven into the annals of the lifeboat service. The west wall of the church is hung with boards commemorating in some detail the achievements of Brook's early lifeboat crews. Every year throughout the month of August the Isle of Wight Natural History and Archaeological Society stage a most interesting and informative exhibition 'Local Look', in Brook's village hall. So if you are tempted into this short diversion to the village I will see you later!

Turn right and cross a cattle grid opposite the Brook road, and go along the rough drive towards the old lifeboat station. If those walls could speak what tales would be told! That small bark thrust into a violent sea; then driven by wind or might of muscle to some stricken vessel, by dauntless men whose last thoughts were of self. And what unfeeling owner could remove the roof of so sacred a place — to improve his view? Should not such a building be 'listed' by virtue of services rendered whether or not it has architectural merit? — for no less than 263 lives were saved during the 76 years (until 1936) of Brook's lifeboat service.

Go off half-left just before the lifeboat house and head towards a seat and a stile at the clifftop. You then have a succession of about 5 stiles, and all the while a fine view inland. The undulations on the otherwise smoothly rounded summit of the down behind Brook are burial mounds dating back to Bronze Age times. They are usually mapped as 'The Five Barrows'. I have counted seven but the official records give eight. As with many archaeological sites the barrows have been molested by thoughtless 'treasure' seekers. These vandals may destroy valuable historical evidence, with negligible gain to themselves. The beach to the west of Chilton Chine (which you are now approaching) has a very special place in the world of Palaentology. It is here that a total of 26 dinosaur footprints were discovered in 1977 on sandstone ledges on the foreshore. A number of these prints were removed — rock and all — and placed in Sandown Museum. Revealed by the scavenging sea they would otherwise fall prey to the same sea, and be lost forever.

When you arrive at Chilton Chine don't go down into the chine (you may find yourself without a path on the far side) but turn left and go across a small car park to the road. Turn right in the road and go forward to a footpath just beyond Chilton Chine Holiday Centre. This path follows the extremity of the Centre and places you back on the cliff path. Before long you will pass the seaward side of Brighstone Holiday Centre. With the passage of time the chalets get nearer to the sea as the cliff falls away piece by piece. The Centre's original holding of 18 acres — back in 1931 when it first opened — has been reduced to about 7: a vivid illustration of the way in which the Island is shrinking. According to a local geologist the Island could all but disappear in the space of 1000 years!

And now to Grange Chine — immediately beyond Grange Chine Camp Site. The Chine once owned the distinction (shared with its neighbour at Brook) of being home of the first lifeboat station on the Island. The boathouse stood close to the mouth of the chine on a ledge now occupied by a group of caravans. Throughout its outstanding career from 1860 to 1915 the station was responsible for saving 433 lives. Its very first call was on April 2nd 1862. The barque Cedarine, on her maiden voyage from Bermuda to Portsmouth with 191 time-expired convicts on board, was wrecked close to the lifeboat station. After a short spell of freedom the convicts were rounded up by the militia.

The hazards of the sea were very real in those days, with tragedy often close at hand. On March 9th 1888 the coxswain and second coxswain died when the lifeboat was taken out to the full-rigged ship Sirenia, wrecked on the Atherfield Ledge. A stone in Brighstone Churchyard commemorates the heroism of these men.

To terminate to-day's walk you should follow the path as it curves inland immediately before Grange Chine. This will place the chine on your right and Grange Farm Camp Site on your left. A rough drive will then take you on the final leg to the Military Road, where you will have the welcome sight of a bus stop! (If, however, you are set on reaching Blackgang today you should go down the drive to the footbridge at the mouth of the chine and then turn to **(7)** on page 25). Brighstone village is quite close now — about ½ mile inland from the Military Road. Although marred by a large gaudy tea garden the village is worth visiting for its Church and its cottages (and for the *other* tea garden). A notable achievement in the life of the church, and one that is echoed in the name of the public house, is that three of its rectors later became bishops. Bishop Ken of Bath and Wells, author of a number of well-known hymns, was rector from 1666 to 1670. Bishop Wilberforce, who was rector from 1830 to 1840, is remembered more for his immediate ancestry than for himself: his father William Wilberforce was the prime-mover in the abolition of slavery in the British colonies. The memorial stone that I mentioned earlier — the one recording the bravery of two Brighstone lifeboatmen — can be seen beside the path leading to the lower gate of the churchyard. Do go inside the church; you will find it both refreshing and beautiful. And do have a look at North Street.

Returning to Freshwater Bay
Bus 46 (summer only) from Grange Bridge.
Bus 28 or 29 from Brighstone (infrequent, summer only).

Accommodation
Buddlebrook Guest House, Brighstone. Tel. (0983) 740381.
Hunninghall Guest House, Hunnyhill, Brighstone. Tel. (0983) 740484.
Chilton Farm House (nr. Chilton Chine). Tel. (0983) 740338.
Fishers Brook, Rectory Lane, Brighstone. Tel. (0983) 740308.

Refreshments available at Freshwater Bay, Shippards Chine, Brook and Brighstone.

3. GRANGE TO BLACKGANG

DISTANCE: 6 miles (9.7km)

CAR PARKING at Grange On the grass verge beside the A3055 Military Road. And it's legal!

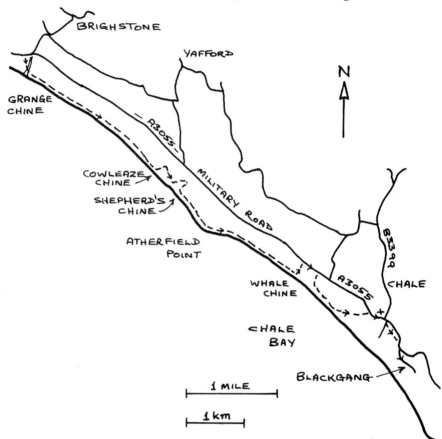

This should be another easy-going day along the cliff edge of south-west Wight. St. Catherine's Hill, topped by the Oratory (an old lighthouse) and Rocken End at the penultimate southern tip of the Island, dominates the view more and more as we proceed. This coast is notorious in the annals of seafaring — notorious for the great number of wrecks that have occurred here over the centuries, particularly in the days of sail. Many a fine vessel has fallen prey to the dreaded Atherfield Ledge (which is about half-way along today's walk) as if coaxed onto the rocks by some mysterious and compelling force.

Immediately opposite the Brighstone turn-off from the A3055 Military Road (at grid reference 420820 and not far from Barney's Road House) a rough drive-cum-public footpath leads to Grange Farm Caravan Site and to the coast. Proceed along this until you reach a small group of permanent caravans sited close to the cliff edge. At this point what is now a grassy path curves left and downhill to meet a footbridge over the mouth of Grange Chine.

(7) Looking inland you now have a good view of the chine, with Grange Bridge at its head. The bridge (more correctly a viaduct) was constructed in the 1860's with bricks made and baked on site and had a purely military function. The public did not have legal access to this or the Military Road until 1933. It is at this vulnerable point that 19th-century troops were stationed to ward off any possible 'enemy' incursion when relations with our neighbours across the Channel were a bit touchy.

As mentioned in the previous chapter, dinosaurs once walked the Wealden Beds that are now exposed along this coast. In the late 1970's a stir of excitement surrounded the discovery of a single dinosaur bone here in Brighstone Bay. This was from a Diplodocus dinosaur which would have approached the formidable length of 100 feet. Diplodocus is normally associated with North America and the 'find' may be the first of its kind in Europe. Now we must be on our way!

After less than ¼ mile along the cliff edge (at a stile) a path runs inland (to another stile); here a sign post points to Brighstone. But that is for information only; so don't go down there! Eventually you will have a fairly steep climb up to what is clearly the highest point along this stretch of coast (with a steep drop seaward: so take care). The next port of call is Cowleaze Chine, where things can get a little complicated. Go inland just before the chine, keeping a large chalet (fronted by a flagpole) on your right and a ditch on your left. After crossing a camp site you will meet a rough drive that crosses the head of the chine. Don't proceed as far as the toilet building ahead (even if you are desperate — it's for campers only) but double back on the other side of the chine, so that it will be on your immediate right. Advance alongside the chine to a pair of stiles (one on each side of a ditch) at the far right-hand corner of the field that you are now in. Once over these stiles cross the next field to a stile in its far right-hand corner (at a signpost), then go steeply down into Shepherd's Chine — handrail provided! Follow the chine inland until you meet a coast-path signpost. Turn right here and cross the chine, passing a 'works' building on your right. Then climb up the far side of the chine, keeping right at a Y-junction near the top. Follow the chine in the seaward direction back to the cliff edge.

When you pass (in the distance) a terrace of coastguard cottages you will be above the notorious Atherfield Point, graveyard of many fine ships. A galaxy of ships names is invisibly engraved on the rocks here: Atlas, Alcester, Auguste, Dolly, Diligent, Duke of Westminster, Eider, Sirenia; these and more spent their final agonising moments in this tragic place. The first recorded wreck was in 1314. This was the 'St. Mary', laden with 174 'tuns' of white wine (I make that 43,848 gallons!) belonging to the Monastery of Livers in Picardy. The ship became a complete wreck, but the crew — and the wine — was recovered. Walter de Godeton, the Lord of the Manor, was found guilty of unlawfully obtaining some of the wine. As a penalty he was ordered to pay for the wine and to build a lighthouse on St. Catherine's Hill. The lighthouse had an oratory attached where a priest 'trimmed the light' and sang masses for those lost at sea. In 1785 a new lighthouse was started but never completed. The two lighthouses ('Salt Pot' and 'Mustard Pot') stand to this day on St. Catherine's Hill and are in view directly ahead. The Mustard Pot has a large transformer inside and an aerial mast outside — an unfortunate inheritance for a Listed Ancient Monument.

Continuing along the path and glancing down the cliff face you should see the winding gear used to haul small fishing boats part-way up from the shore. The days when large shoals of mackerel coasted into Chale Bay are long-gone. At present the catch is mostly lobster. The next variation in the path is at the spectacular Whale Chine where you should go inland to meet the road. This chine was christened in 1924 when a 49-foot whale became stranded on the beach (or so I'm told!) When the chine meets the road it (the chine) promptly turns right and follows the road for some distance. You should do likewise until you reach a footpath on the right just beyond a small car park. This will lead you back to the cliff path.

Your next chine — Walpen — will steer you inland towards Chale. Don't be tempted to jump this chine when it narrows to a fissure. It's deep; and you might end up in the wrong place — in more ways than one! So persevere until you reach a footbridge over the chine. Cross this, turn left immediately and follow the chine (which is now no more than a ditch) inland along its right-hand edge.

You may be puzzled at our departure from the cliff edge. This is necessary because the coast path has completely 'gone over the side' ½ mile further on where it once passed the seaward end of Cliff Terrace, Blackgang. More of Cliff Terrace later.

You should see Chale Church directly ahead, and Michael Hoy's monument at the northern end of St. Catherine's Hill. The monument was put up by Hoy to commemorate a visit of the Czar in 1814, but later inscribed (ironically) to the English who fell in the Crimean War. It's a

Chale Church

very fine walk from the old lighthouse to Hoy's Monument along the crest of the Down, by the way. When the ditch curves right it is crossed by a footbridge. Go over this to a stile, and then along the right-hand edge of a field to the Military Road. Turn right in the road and go along this to the Church of St. Andrew at Chale.

The church is solemnly linked with a tragic event that occurred along this 'violent coast' on 11th October, 1836. The 345 ton 'Clarendon' was driven ashore at Blackgang by a heavy storm. Only three of her complement of 24 passengers and crew survived and only through the bravery of a hardy fisherman, John Wheeler. Supported by a line from the shore he went down into the seething foam and brought back three men. Moments later the 'Clarendon' became a complete wreck and the 21 others still on board perished. Most of these unfortunate victims were

The Clarendon victims, Chale Churchyard

buried here in Chale Churchyard. The word 'Clarendon', faintly visible on a large tombstone just north of the church, bears silent witness to that terrible day. Out of this tragedy came the decision to build a fine new lighthouse at St. Catherine's Point; but more of that tomorrow. The box tombs to the south of the church are said to have been used for concealing contraband brandy, in the days when smuggling was commonplace on the Island. Finally, before I let you go, Chale possesses what was once considered to be one of the most interesting domestic buildings on the Island. This is Chale Abbey Farmhouse, which is not far away in Upper House Lane.

From Chale Church go forward (eastward) for a short distance, in the Military Road and turn first right into The Terrace. Go along this for about 100 yards to a footpath on the left signposted to Blackgang. If your curiosity is anything like mine you will want to venture further along this road to its far end at the cliff edge. Over the years the cliff has worked its way inland taking road and houses with it; and residents continue to live right up to the brink — well almost! Now back to that Blackgang footpath. This will take you between hedges and up to meet the road. Turn right here and go forward to the junction of the old with the new coast road. The old road (the right-hand branch) was severed in 1928 when a vast amount of cliff crashed seaward. There's enough of it left (at the time of writing) to take you as far as Blackgang Chine, where again your curiosity may take you a little further — to the blunt end of the road.

Once the shock of car parks, coaches and cafes has subsided you should seriously consider paying your way through the turnstile; on a quiet day the Chine can be quite pleasant, and you stand to learn something about wrecks, dinosaurs and the Wild West! The Sawmill Museum opposite the Chine was once a barn, then a stable, then a dwelling; but never a sawmill! Blackgang is more than a Chine and a Sawmill Museum: it is remembered in the annals of the Island's military history as the site of the very first World War II casualty — a rabbit.

A bus may be boarded here for Niton; then from Niton it's a pleasant walk up to Whitwell Youth Hostel. Get off the bus at the junction of Church Street with Newport Road; then cross Newport Road to Rectory Road. Go along Rectory Road to the first turning on the right — Allotment Road (N.B. *not* Rectory Lane) when Allotment Road turns left go with it through a housing estate to its very end. The road divides at a row of older houses; take the left-hand branch leading to a field. Cross the field to a wooden gate directly ahead and go forward in a narrow path. This soon joins a track starting from Current Cottage. The Youth Hostel is at the far end of the track.

Returning to Grange or Freshwater Bay
Bus 46 (summer only).

Accommodation
Cedar Crest, Chale. Tel. Chale Green 280.
Seafield, off Blythe Shute, Chale. Tel. (0983) 730515.
The White House, Blackgang. Tel. (0983) 730332.
The Halls, Chale Green. Tel. Chale Green 267.
Cortina, Gotten Lane, Chale. Tel. Chale Green 292.
Youth Hostel, Whitwell. Tel. (0983) 730473 (closed on Thursdays and some Wednesdays, except during July and August).

Refreshments available at Brighstone, Atherfield Bay Holiday Centre and Blackgang.

4. BLACKGANG TO VENTNOR

DISTANCE: 5.5 miles (8.9km)

CAR PARKS at Blackgang (1) Directly opposite the Chine entrance.
(2) Viewpoint car park overlooking Blackgang — beside the A3055, and free!

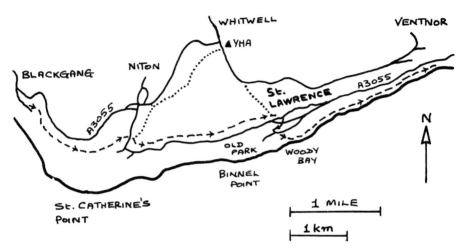

The steep climb up from Blackgang to Gore Cliff makes a dramatic start to today's walk. Once there the path stays at the upper level as far as High Hat above St. Lawrence, all the while offering a fine view of the Undercliff below. The earlier official route kept to the upper cliff all the way to Ventnor. This has been modified from High Hat onwards and now includes the lovely village of St. Lawrence and the fine undulating lower cliff between Woody Bay and Ventnor.

If you are launching off from the viewpoint car park above Blackgang you should proceed along the footpath that runs seaward towards the cliff; then turn left into the cliff path. Continue from **(8)** below. Otherwise, passing the entrance to Blackgang Chine on your right, turn left into the car park opposite the Ship Ashore Inn. Then turn right into the upper half of the car park and go uphill to its far right-hand corner. Here a flight of ten steps lead up to a stile; this is followed by a short narrow path to a field. Go uphill along the right-hand edge of the field to a stile in its top right-hand corner, and up again to a seat overlooking the cliff — Gore Cliff. Ignore the path running inland here **(8)** and go straight on along the cliff edge. You now have the best view possible (from the cliff path) of the 'Salt Pot' and 'Mustard Pot', the two lighthouses on St. Catherine's

Hill. Their story was outlined yesterday (see page 26) when we were at Atherfield Point. The Salt Pot looks for all the world like a rocket ready for lift-off. Early Man also put St. Catherine's Hill to good use, evidenced by the extensive cultivation terraces on its south-west slope and the occurrence of burial mounds elsewhere on the Hill. Excavation of one of these mounds in 1926 revealed the skeleton of a 'Beaker' man who died in his thirties, 3500 years ago. All in all a very interesting hill, and worth a visit all to itself.

Down in the jumbled landscape of the Undercliff you will see (before long) a car park marking the termination of the Undercliff Road which, until 26th July 1928, continued to Blackgang. On that day a mass of rock estimated at 200,000 tons, fell away from the cliff (just about where you are now) wiping out the Undercliff Road for good. By the following month the pent-up energy in what had become a very unstable landmass, was released in a veritable glacier of rocks, clay and water, gouging its way down to Rocken End and into the sea. The incident generated so much excitement that special excursions from London were organised for those wanting to see the 'slip' in action.

It may go without saying that the Undercliff — with its tangle of vegetation and southerly aspect — is much favoured by the butterfly population. However, not everyone will be aware that this is the only place in the British Isles where the Granville Fritillary can be found. That's quite staggering — to my mind!

You should soon have an excellent view of the 'new' St. Catherine's Lighthouse down there on the lower cliff. Construction of this 'light' started in 1838 following the tragic wreck of the Clarendon two years earlier (see page 27). It has not been without tragedy of its own, however: three lighthouse keepers were killed during a German air raid in the Second World War. Knowles Farm, to the right of the lighthouse, is where Marconi established his second experimental wireless station on the Island. This was in 1902 and superceded the Alum Bay station mentioned in our first walk. The farmhouse is now in the care of the National Trust and is used for self-catering holidays. All very nice, I should think, except when those fog horns are blowing.

Continuing straight on, you will soon go over a stile and pass to the right of the 'Post Office Automatic Radio Station', with five masts. Then over two stiles, one at each end of a field, the second leading to a downhill path under trees. This is Boxers Lane, renowned for its badger setts. The path becomes a rough drive and soon turns left to join the Niton road. Turn right in the road and go downhill for about 15 yards to a drive on the left. Follow this up for short distance to a signpost pointing to St. Lawrence. (This is a convenient break-off point for those going to

31

Whitwell Youth Hostel; directions are given at the end of the chapter). Turn right at the signpost and go alongside a stone wall towards the entrance to a house called 'Longstock'. Just before the entrance go left and uphill along a footpath under trees. This will lead you back to the cliff path. Keep straight on now, avoiding all paths going off left and right. About ½ mile from your crossing of the Niton Road, you will see the curved bay which is Puckaster Cove. This, according to all the guide books, is where King Charles II landed in 1675, when he was driven ashore in a gale.

Through a gap in the hedge further along you should be able to discern Binnel Point and Spindler's Folly. In 1883, an industrialist William Spindler aspired to a grandiose scheme for populating his Undercliff estate with roads, people and a harbour — a whole new town in fact. The project was abandoned six years later, at his death. Spindler's Folly (the sea wall) remains, but only as stranded lumps of stone torn apart by the sea. When you reach the next summit of the path you will have quite a good view of Spindler's manor house 'Old Park' situated about ¼ mile north-east of Binnel Point. Find the swimming pool and you're there! The house is now a hotel, while the estate accommodates the Tropical Bird Park and Isle of Wight Glass. From this summit you also have your first view of Ventnor and its pier. Aerial masts proliferate: the two coming up on your left are part of a British Telecom transmitting station while the two inland on Stenbury Down are used for aircraft communication (or so they were in my day). Directly ahead on St. Boniface Down the radar scanners are rotating on behalf of the Civil Aviation Authority.

As you approach the two aerial masts a stile will usher you into the open and down a grassy slope to a footpath signpost and a seat. (This is another convenient point from which to break off for Whitwell Youth Hostel. For this go inland to a stile at a break in the hedge, then forward along a drive to its junction with the Whitwell road. Turn left there and follow the road to Whitwell. The hostel is in the lovely old vicarage next to the Church).

Now back to the signpost and that seat, which, believe it or not, is situated almost directly over a 619 yard-long tunnel! This was used by the old Isle of Wight Central Railway when it ran trains from Merstone to Ventnor West Station. A bell would sound to announce the presence of a train in the tunnel; then as the train emerged it would make a left-hand turn before steaming its way along the Undercliff to Ventnor. Engine drivers would often make brief stops so that passengers could enjoy the magnificent view. The last train to run along this line was the 7.57 p.m. from Ventnor West on 13th September 1952. It was a sad day indeed because it marked the beginning of the end for the Island's railway network. Now, whatever you do, don't go looking for the tunnel exit: the cliff is very hazardous from this level.

We now follow the new Coast Path route down through St. Lawrence and along the lower cliff to Ventnor. The earlier route along the upper cliff enjoyed only a limited view of the coast and had the company of a road for much of its length. Some maps (and signposts) may indicate this earlier route; so to avoid confusion I suggest that you follow my directions unswervingly from now on (as if you haven't already!).

From the signpost and seat go seaward and downhill in a sunken path. Passing another seat on the left continue down to meet Seven Sisters' Road — crossing the former railway trackbed near the bottom. Turn left in Seven Sisters' Road and go along this to the first turning on the right, Spindler's Road; but if you possess even the slightest interest in old railways you should delay going down Spindler's Road and continue instead along Seven Sisters' Road for less than ¼ mile. There you will find St. Lawrence's old railway station, now a private house but looking very much as it did in its heyday. Having gone that far along Seven Sisters do go a little further to the Old Church. This was the smallest church in England until extended in 1842. It also served the smallest parish — less than 350 acres.

Back at the junction of Seven Sisters' with Spindler's Road, go down Spindler's (there's a shop and a Post Office tucked away on the left, by the way) and cross Undercliff Drive (by St. Lawrence Inn) to Old Park Road. Follow this downhill — ignoring Hunts Road on the right — to its junction with Woolverton Road at the bottom, where a sign points to the Old Park Hotel, Tropical Bird Park and Isle of Wight Glass. Turn left into Woolverton Road and go along this for 70 yards to a gate on the right

Woody Bay

just beyond a house called 'Gazebo' (of all things!). Go through the gate, downhill to a stile, and straight on across a field — with a wire fence on your immediate right. Turn right in a rough drive at the far end of the field and go along this for a short distance to a signpost. Turn left here and aim for the highest of two stiles. You are now on the lower cliff path, with Woody Bay on your right and little to hinder progress from here to Ventnor.

The poet Alfred Noyes had the good fortune to spend almost 30 years of his life at St. Lawrence. His home, Lisle Combe, can be seen from the coast path a few hundred yards after passing a large pond. Look for a large stone house with pale blue timber-work and no less than 18 ornate chimneys.

Soon after this a wide upward-sloping green ushers in the lovely Botanic Garden: an excellent place to take refreshment and to enjoy summer flowers and exotic greenery. There is little to remind visitors of the National Hospital for Diseases of the Chest that stood here for 100 years until 1968. The hospital was founded by Dr. Arthur Hassall following considerable interest in the curative effects of Ventnor's climate. The hospital was linked to the cliff by a tunnel which was used for the disposal of kitchen left-overs. Its closed-off entrance can still be seen from inside the present Botanic Gardens. You will need to stretch your neck rather dangerously for a glimpse of the exit: this is half-way up the cliff at a point almost directly in line with a small ivy clad brick building (a hospital incinerator) on the inland edge of the sloping green.

Immediately beyond the 'incinerator', where the green narrows and slopes downhill, the path itself runs uphill to skirt the upper edge of the Botanic Garden. Go straight on from the far end of the Garden (where a signpost points left to the Smuggling Museum) and, after passing a cricket green on the left, forward along a tarmac drive. Not far beyond Flowerbrook Tea Garden (my annual place of pilgrimage) and almost into Ventnor, a choice of ways presents itself. Take the lower, easier branch; the upper would simply lead you back to the lower, eventually.

From Niton to Whitwell Youth Hostel

Where the gravel drive turns right to follow a stone wall, go forward into a bridleway signposted to Whitwell (NT26). This soon divides two ways. Take the left-hand branch (the level one) running behind a row of bungalows and houses. At a junction of paths just beyond the houses keep straight on along a path signposted to Whitwell. This leads to Allotment Road (the two left-hand paths leaving that 'junction' lead into Niton's attractive village centre). Turn right into Allotment Road and go through a housing estate to its very end. The road divides at a row of older houses; take the left-hand branch leading to a field. Cross the field to a wooden gate directly ahead and go forward in a narrow path. This soon joins a track starting from Current Cottage. The Youth Hostel is at the far end of the track.

Returning to Blackgang
Bus routes 16/16B, 46 (46 summer only; 16/16B infrequent in winter).

Accommodation
Dudley House, Dudley Road, Ventnor. Tel. (0983) 853386.
Harborne Court Hotel, Spring Gardens, Ventnor. Tel. (0983) 852048.
Clarens Guest House, 33 Alpine Road, Ventnor. Tel. (0983) 852045.
Fairways, Undercliff Drive, St. Lawrence. Tel. (0983) 852091.

Refreshments available at Blackgang, Ventnor Botanic Gardens, Steephill, Ventnor.

5. VENTNOR TO SANDOWN

DISTANCE: 5 miles (8km)

CAR PARKING at Ventnor (1) At the western end of the Esplanade where this joins Bath Road.

(2) At the junction of Spring Hill with High Street — and many more!

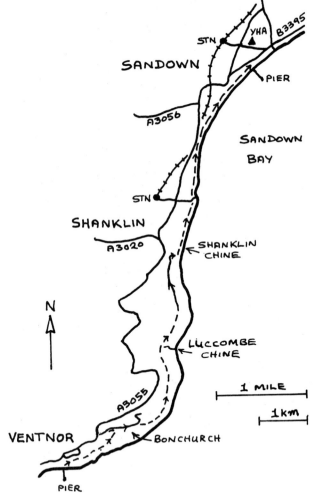

Ventnor, Shanklin, Sandown: three 'honeypots' attracting thousands of visitors each year, a fact which may prompt you to cut this section from your circumnavigation of the Island! But in so doing you will miss the delightful village of Bonchurch — with its many literary associations; also the wooded Landslip and Luccombe Cliffs, and the option of a steep but exhilarating descent to Luccombe Chine.

Once again I will warn of possible confusion from reading earlier maps: the route described here replaces two predecessors which started from the site of Ventnor's old railway station — in its elevated position north of the town.

Now I hesitate to start you off from the seafront because the route up from there (across the Cascade) may well have changed by the time of your visit. All being well this part of Ventnor will be graced by an enormous glass dome — a 'magic umbrella' under which a whole range of tropical plants will be cultivated. The Cascade itself had a more utilitarian association in earlier days: it was the tailrace for Ventnor's corn mill. The mill stood at the seaward end of what is now Pier Street (above the Cascade) and was demolished in about 1867. So to avoid being caught up in the likely Dome complex we will start at cliff-top level just below the Winter Gardens. Here a tarmac path runs eastward (from the Cascade) and rises to meet a direction indicator and a sheltered seat. Stay in the path as it runs alongside a stone wall on the left and curves left to join an ascending flight of steps. From the top of the steps go across a car park and join Dudley Road on the far side. Turning right here you will soon meet Victoria Street coming in from the left. Turn right into this and, ignoring Wheeler's Bay Road on the right, follow it through (it now becomes St. Catherines Street) to join Madeira Road. Going forward in Madeira Road (avoiding Kings Bay Road and Madeira Vale) you will eventually turn hairpin left and downhill to meet Bonchurch Village Road. Turn right into this and go forward to the village.

Bonchurch Pond on the left is successor to a swampy osier bed where in earlier days willow was harvested for use in the making and mending of crab and lobster pots. Peacock Vane Hotel — also on the left — is noted for its association with Joan Wolfenden, author of three (at least!) excellent books for home and garden.

When the road curves left and uphill (Bonchurch Shute) go straight on into a 'No Through Road' signposted to Winterbourne Hotel. East Dene directly ahead is where the poet Swinburne spent much of his childhood. From East Dene follow the road down to Winterbourne Hotel and the Old Church. Charles Dickens rented Winterbourne from July to October 1849. Not an outstanding revelation, except that it was here that Dickens wrote six chapters of his novel David Copperfield.

The beauty of the Old Church will speak for itself as you contemplate its ancient walls and muse over its time-honoured churchyard. A short descriptive guide is available from the church; it was written in 1931 by

Henry de Vere Stacpoole, a resident of Bonchurch for many years and author of the best-selling novel The Blue Lagoon.

With the church on your right go forward into a path signposted to The Landslip and Shanklin (not the one that passes the east end of the church). This very soon turns half-right to follow the edge of a sports field. Ignore a path leading down to the shore from the far end of the sports field and continue forward alongside Carrigdene Farm. The path now twists and heaves its way through the Landslip with the occasional assistance of stone steps thoughtfully sited. You will pass a signpost showing the direction to Smugglers Haven Cafe (not on our route!) and go under a stand of fine knarled oaks. And you will have the opportunity to relax on a Wishing Seat. Quite a day! The path finally breaks out into the open and joins a drive at Rose Cliff Lodge.

Go straight on down the drive (ignoring a branch on the left) to Dunnose Cottage Restaurant. When the drive soon turns left go forward into the National Trust's Luccombe Cliffs. If time is on your side the diversion from here down to Luccombe Chine is well-worth the 235 steps it takes to get there! The Chine is completely wild and unspoilt; even the fishermen's cottages that once graced the lower levels have disappeared. A chapel that served the cottagers was moved lock, stock and barrel to the top of the cliff. This can still be seen — if you know where to look. In 1946 the bones of a gigantic Sauropod dinosaur were found on the beach near the Chine; so while you are down there it might pay to be observant!

Now back to Luccombe Cliffs. Here a gravel path takes you through a pleasant area of trees and scrub and alongside the conveniently-sited Luccombe Tea Garden; then on to a road at the far end of the 'Cliffs'. Going along the road you should soon have a view of Shanklin's pier before descending what I refer to as "that agonising hill" (from the time when I walked with my family in the reverse direction — with heavy rucksacks!). When you are nearly at the bottom of the hill (Luccombe Road) you are met by Rylestone Gardens (a public park) on the right, and, coming in from the left, rear, Popham Road. You now have a choice of routes through Shanklin. The 'official' one alongside Rylestone Gardens involves a zig-zag descent to the shore, followed by a very short walk along the shore and a zig-zag back up again! This will place you on Keats Green; and you will miss the town altogether. The alternative is to continue straight on into Shanklin, approaching Keats Green by a level route — much easier, and a chance to shop and see something of the town. Under the assumption that most walkers will wish to go into the town, I have relegated the official route to the end of the chapter.

So with all that over, go forward into the tarmac path under trees, (Chine Hollow) and cross the footbridge beside the entrance to Shanklin

Chine. If Blackgang Chine was something of a disappointment you should find ample compensation here. According to the brochure it is ". . . a world of enchanting vistas and great natural beauty — a former haunt of smugglers and a rich haven of rare plants." A Nature Trail has been prepared by the Isle of Wight Natural History and Archaeological Society; so it must be good. From the Chine entrance it's but a short distance to Shanklin Old Village, now very much part of the town, and a world of tea gardens and gift shops. The American poet Henry Wadsworth Longfellow (1807-82) considered Shanklin 'one of the greatest and loveliest places in the Kingdom'. Times change! An inscription written by Longfellow appears on the 'fountain' at the junction of Chine Hollow with High Street. The poet John Keats stayed at 76 High Street (Eglantine Cottage) in the summer of 1819. The 'cottage' is still there, but it is now a hotel.

Go along Chine Avenue (which is first on the right after you join High Street from Shanklin Chine) and then along Chine Road to the cliff top adjacent to Keats Green. **(9)** As you go along Keats Green you will have sight of three very attractive Victorian shelters down on the esplanade; also a fine clocktower commemorating Queen Victoria's Jubilee in 1897.

Continuing straight on you will join the Eastcliff Prom just before The Lift. The Lift was built in 1956 to replace the earlier version of 1891. Remnants of the old lift are still visible beneath the new; and where a closed-off flight of steps clings to the cliff a faded notice proclaims: "The nearest way to Esplanade, down the lift, one penny". If you pay today's fare and descend to the lower level you can learn something of PLUTO — not the Disney character but the code name for the World War II project 'Pipeline Under The Ocean'. The Lift played a vital part in a complex system of pumps and pipelines which had the sole function of supplying motor spirit to the invasion forces across the Channel. "Pipe left from here" is the proud boast written on a wall in the lower lift house — the starting point of its journey under the Channel to the French coast at Cherbourg.

The next feature of interest down there on the esplanade is a large red corrugated-iron roof covering an amusement arcade. The building started life as a seaplane hanger in Bembridge Harbour during the First World War. It was moved here in 1923.

It's now a straight cliff walk all the way to Sandown, with only three interruptions from me. The first is to point out the fine stone building, Winchester House, beside the path at Lake — midway between Shanklin and Sandown. This is a Church of England Holiday Centre accommodating up to 116 guests. It was built in 1898. Secondly; you may chance to see a London Underground train passing close-by. This line originally ran all the way from Ryde to Ventnor, but is now unfortunately cut short at

Shanklin. Although the underground stock was brought to the Island at great expense, there has been a strong call to bring back steam locomotion to this line as a tourist attraction. I wish the idea every success. And thirdly: Sandown Battery Gardens are on your left just before you make the final descent. The Battery dates back to the 1860's (when it was fitted with four seven-inch Armstrong guns) and abandoned shortly after the First World War.

Now if your first impression of Sandown is not entirely complimentary, be reassured: there is more than shops, amusement arcades and sandy beaches. Sandown has an interesting geological museum above the public library in High Street; and it has two notable literary associations: Charles Darwin started work on his Origin of Species here (at the Kings Head Hotel — now the gabled part of Ocean Hotel), and Lewis Carroll lodged in High Street. There is also an excellent Youth Hostel. This is in Fitzroy Street and can be reached from the pier by going up Pier Street and crossing High Street into Melville Street. Fitzroy Street is first on the right. More fascinating facts about Sandown tomorrow!

'Official' route from Rylestone Gardens to Keats Green, Shanklin

Go along the road beside Rylestone Gardens — to its end adjacent to a Cheshire Home. A paved path takes over from here and leads to the cliff edge where a zig-zag path descends the cliff face. Turn left when on the beach and go along this for a close pass of the Old Fisherman's Cottage. The cottage is now a 'Free House' devoted to the sport of eating and drinking. You will find an uphill zig-zag route starting mid-way between the lower chine entrance and the public toilets. This will take you up to Keats Green at the top of the cliff. Now back to **(9)** on page 39.

Returning to Ventnor
Bus routes 16/16B, 46 (46 summer only)

Accommodation
Marine Villa Guest House, 16 York Road, Sandown. Tel. (0983) 405337.
Moncoffer Guest House, 26 Melville Street, Sandown. Tel. (0983) 405410.
Kensington Guest House, Station Road, Sandown. Tel. (0983) 406235.
Penmartyn Guest House, Station Road, Sandown. Tel. (0983) 403449.
Linden House, 23 York Road, Sandown. Tel. (0983) 404684.
Youth Hostel, Fitzroy Street, Sandown. Tel. (0983) 402651. Closed Mondays, except during July and August; also Tuesdays Oct.-March.

Refreshments available at Ventnor, Luccombe Cliffs, Shanklin, Sandown.

6. SANDOWN TO BEMBRIDGE

DISTANCE: 6 miles (9.7km)

CAR PARKING at Sandown (1) Roadside parking along the Esplanade (free!)

(2) Numerous car parks along the coast road (Culver Parade) east of the town.

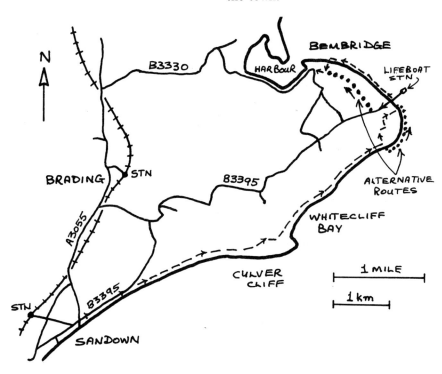

Today's walk includes something of a climax as the path ascends the magnificent Culver Down — the last coastal highpoint this end of the Island. The path descends the north-east slope of the Down and reaches sea level 1½ miles further on at Foreland. Thereafter it is a low-level course all the way to Bembridge Harbour — the attractive yachting centre at the eastern extremity of the Island. Where the walking is right down on the shore itself and subject to the vicissitudes of the sea, I have given directions for two short diversions, so that you can avoid the hazards of 'coasteering' and arrive in Bembridge with dry feet.

Since the Pier is probably the easiest of Sandown's landmarks to find I will start you off from there. So from the pier go eastward along the Esplanade to where it turns left just beyond Sandringham Hotel. The road very soon joins a five-way junction, overlooked by Sandown's public library. The Museum of Geology is situated on the floor above the library and is certainly worth visiting. Although quite small, the Museum houses an interesting collection of geological and palaeontological specimens. At the 5-way junction turn right into Culver Parade (the B3395) and head towards the distant Culver Cliff.

Sandown Zoo is housed in the old granite fort just beyond the Grand Hotel. The fort was completed in 1866 and formed a link in a chain of defences designed to counteract the threat of French invasion. During the Second World War the fort duplicated Shanklin Lift as a pumping station for PLUTO — 'Pipeline Under The Ocean'. Vital fuel supplies were pumped from here to the Allied Forces across the Channel.

Leave the road when it curves inland to Yaverland and go straight on across the adjacent public car park. The path climbs gently uphill from the far end of the car park, passing Sandown Bay Holiday Centre on the left. The Centre is on a site previously occupied by Yaverland Fort, of which very little remains. The coast along here is noted for its outcrop of Wealden Marls, a clayey sediment in which fossilised dinosaur bones are occasionally discovered. The fact that Yaverlandia is the name of a particular species of dinosaur underlines the importance of the area in palaentological circles. The naming arose from the discovery on these Yaverland cliffs of a small fragment of skull belonging to a previously unknown dinosaur type. It could just be an awful lot has been made of an awful little!

Wreck Post

Continuing uphill you will pass a tall white post fitted with triangular 'steps'. This 'wreck post' is designed to simulate the mast of a distressed ship during breeches-buoy rescue practice. In real life a line is fired from the cliff to the stricken vessel; the line is then anchored to the ship's mast and the crew hauled in to the safety of the cliff.

A stile and gate ahead marks the mid-point of a level section of the path. Here a fine hedge of hawthorn trees (very beautiful when in bloom) goes off half-left. Next you will pass between two metal posts (all that's left of an old gate) before meeting a stile at an indent in the coast. Don't go over the stile but continue straight on up the steep slope. When the path divides into two almost immediately take the right-hand branch; this keeps fairly close to a wire fence on the right. The Earl of Yarborough's obelisk and a terrace of coastguard cottages should now be coming into view. When these are within a few hundred yards you should aim your sights at a gate midway between them in the far left-hand corner of a 'field' (if I can call it that). The gate leads on to a drive; turn right in this and left through a kissing gate after a few paces. (A left hand turn in the track will take you to Bembridge Fort — if you are so inclined (see page 48). The path now continues across Culver Down midway between the obelisk and Culver Haven Hotel.

After a short pause to read the Earl's inscription go downhill towards Whitecliff Bay, roughly in the direction of an ugly caravan site and twice passing under electricity wires. You will reach a stile at a short distance downhill. Go over this and along a level path (between damaged wire fences) to two stiles directly ahead. Your stile is the left-hand of the two; the one directly ahead leads into a National Trust car park situated behind Culver Battery. The battery's Second World War gun emplacements are still there and command a fine view of the Channel. Go over

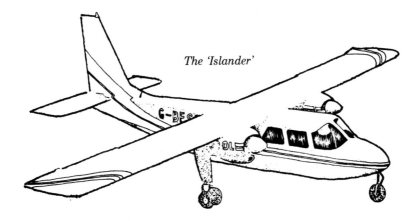

The 'Islander'

that left-hand stile and downhill in a chalky path to another stile. The view inland includes Bembridge Airport where the popular turbine-powered Islander aircraft are manufactured. There are fears among Island residents that future developments at the airport will cause increased nuisance from aircraft noise. I sympathise.

A scrubby area makes an appearance beyond the stile, followed by a few discreetly sited chalets. Beyond the chalets a short length of the path has fallen away; hence the new footbridge. Continue downhill along the right-hand border of the caravan site and on to a footbridge over a concreted gulley (for want of a better description) not omitting to glance back at the fine cliffs overlooking Whitecliff Bay. Next you have a rough path running ahead into a wood; when the path divides into two inside the wood (beside a small concrete block) take the right-hand branch. A curious earthwork cuts across your route soon after that; this is traversed by a flight of steps up and down. There are more such steps before the path leads you into a sportsfield. Bembridge School stands of the far side of the field.

Few guide books fail to mention that Bembridge School is home to the largest single collection of the work of John Ruskin; but who he was, and what form his 'work' took, is rarely mentioned. In a nutshell, Ruskin, who lived from 1819 to 1900, was a prodigious artist and illustrator and an outstanding writer on art and social reform. The Ruskin Gallery at the school is open to view, but by prior arrangement only.

Go along the right-hand edge of the sports field to join a path leading off from its far right-hand corner. This will take you through a low woodland of thorn and elm and back alongside the sports-field. A short distance along the extremity of the field and you are back under the trees. Once out from under the trees the path turns sharp left. Follow this round for a few paces and then turn right to resume your previous direction parallel to the coast. When the path soon divides into two — before a stand of hawthorn trees — take either branch; they take you under trees and out into the open again. You then have a long level path bordered by fields on the left and low cliffs on the right. At the end of this you will meet the seaward end of a rough drive at Foreland. Cross the end of the drive to a narrow path opposite; this soon leads to a Coastguard Lookout, a seat with a view, and the Crab and Lobster — a good place for tired feet and dry tongues!

When refreshed and rekindled go along the path behind the Coastguard Lookout and join the end of a drive. Then go inland along the drive to a narrow path on the right just beyond the house numbered '27'. This path meets another road at a roundabout. Turn right here and go down the slipway to the beach. Now follows a ¾ mile stretch along the shore to take you almost as far as the Bembridge lifeboat pier. If the sea is too high for comfort, however, I suggest that you turn to the end of the chapter where directions are given for a safe inland diversion — now signposted and mapped as the 'official' route.

The route along the shore is overlooked for much of its length by the grounds of Bembridge Chalet Hotel. Immediately beyond the grounds a short flight of steps will take you back onto the low cliff and then to Bembridge lifeboat pier. (10) The fine Solent class lifeboat 'Jack Shayler and the Lees' is open to public view on certain days of the week. Bembridge's early lifeboats were housed in what is now the inshore lifeboat station close to the pier entrance. One of these, the 'Queen Victoria' (renamed The Ark and dating back to the turn of the century) is still very much alive — as a houseboat in Bembridge Harbour. We shall see her tomorrow.

From the lifeboat pier go along the sea wall towards a green boathouse and private slipway. You now have the prospect of 1 mile along the shore to Bembridge, with the option of a parallel path through woodland for a good part of the way. If, however, the height of the sea is enough to worry you, you should retreat to the pier and follow the inland route given at the end of the chapter. If not, then go up the short flight of concrete steps just beyond the slipway. This leads to a narrow path running parallel to the coast. When the path goes inland turn right and walk down a flight of steps back to the beach. The rocks and pools along here make this one of the most interesting shores on the Island, especially at low tide. It is highly regarded for the variety of its seaweed and for the richness of its marine life.

Bembridge Harbour comes into view as you make your way along the shore (or along the parallel woodland path) and as you tune your eyes for yet another flight of steps. These are sited beyond a large new timber house and can be identified by their being directly in line with St. Helen's Sea Fort. Go up these steps (you could alternatively continue along the beach as far as Bembridge, if you wish) and forward in a rough drive for about 60 yards to a footpath on the right. This is signposted 'Bembridge Point' and takes you between the buildings of Greylands College and on to meet the B3395 road opposite Bembridge Harbour's Pilot Boat Inn.

(11) Up until 1953 it was possible to return to Sandown by train; in that year the branch line from Bembridge to Brading was closed. Bembridge Station stood close to the Pilot Boat Inn in what was then (not surprisingly) Station Road. Its place has been taken by a terrace of modern flats. It was not only the railway that ran to Brading in earlier days, but the sea also, until it was barred by the construction of the harbour wall — the wall which carries the B3395 road to St. Helens.

Inland route from Foreland to Bembridge Lifeboat Pier

Turn left at the roundabout (instead of right to the slipway) and go inland along the road (Paddock Drive) to its T-junction with Farm Close. Turn right into Farm Close and stay with it as it curves left and joins Farm Lane, a rough drive. Leave the drive after about 200 yards and join a footpath on the right. This straight, timber-fenced, path takes you back towards the coast and draws alongside the entrance to Bembridge Chalet Hotel. Cross the drive here and go forward to join the low cliff edge (where steps link the beach to the cliff). Turn left and proceed along the cliff edge to the lifeboat pier. Now back to **(10)** on page 45.

Inland route from Bembridge Lifeboat Pier to Bembridge

With your back to the pier go inland along Lane End Road for ¼ mile to Swains Lane on the right — an unsurfaced lane starting just beyond a house called St. Malo. When Swains Lane meets a tarmac road (Swains Road) on the left, go forward along a gravel path signposted 'Love Lane and High Street' (there is a post-box just here). When this in turn meets the entrance gate to Tyne Hall on the right, keep straight on along a tarmac drive. The drive turns sharp left when adjacent to four private entrance gates (Pitt House and Pitt Corner). Turn left with the drive, then right along a fenced path immediately. This soon connects with a wide, rough drive in the vicinity of Greylands College. Cross to the footpath opposite and go down to the B3395 road adjacent to Bembridge Harbour's Pilot Boat Inn. Now back to **(11)** on page 45.

Returning to Sandown

Bus route 8 (infrequent in winter).

Accommodation

Crab & Lobster, Foreland (on the coast path). Tel. (0983) 872244.
Barfield Hotel, Steyne Road, Bembridge. Tel. (0983) 872294.
Birdham Hotel, Steyne Road, Bembridge. Tel. (0983) 872875 (AA**).
Bembridge House Hotel, High Street, Bembridge. Tel. (0983) 873975.

Refreshments available at Sandown, Culver, Whitecliff Bay, Foreland, Ethel Point (adjacent to Bembridge Lifeboat Pier), and Bembridge.

7. BEMBRIDGE TO RYDE

DISTANCE: 6 miles (9.7km)

CAR PARKING at Bembridge (1) Silver Beach and The Point car parks, south of the harbour.
(2) The Duver National Trust car park, north of the harbour.

The highlights of today's walk are St. Helen's Duver for its natural history interest, Seaview for its attractive streets and yachting activities, Puckpool Park for its military history. Something for everyone — almost! From The Duver to Seaview the walking is inland across fields and along tracks and quiet lanes; from Seaview to Ryde it's a paved or tarmac route alongside the shore, with much of the interest being seaward across Spithead.

Our starting-point is the memorial fountain close to the three-storey 'Royal Spithead Hotel' (now a college annexe) in Harbour Strand south of the harbour. From here we make our way to St. Helen's Duver by circumnavigating the harbour. This is a long walk to cover a short distance; but it is not without interest: there is the old lifeboat to see; also

47

St. Helen's Tide Mill House — followed by an enjoyable stride along the Mill dam. The alternative route to St. Helen's Duver — and one which will save you one mile of walking — is by way of the harbour ferry. This operates during July and August only, from 10.30 a.m. to 5.30 p.m.; but don't depend on it being there at your beck and call, no matter what! Directions that take you from the memorial fountain to the ferry 'embarkation point' can be found at the end of the chapter.

Assuming you are going the long way round, you should move off from the memorial fountain along the B3395 road — with your back to the 'Royal Spithead Hotel'. You will pass Bembridge Sailing Club on the right and various boat builders' yards on the left. You will also have a distant view of Bembridge Fort and the Earl of Yarborough's monument — both on Bembridge Down over to your left. The fort overlooks Sandown Bay and was constructed between 1862 and 1867 by the Palmerston Government. It was designed as a major island stronghold to combat the threat of invasion by French forces. The Earl of Yarborough was the first Commodore of the Royal Yacht Squadron at Cowes.

Included among the many houseboats lining the harbour is The Ark. As mentioned yesterday The Ark was one of Bembridge's early lifeboats and dates back to the turn of the century.

The road crosses a bridge where the River Yar (the 'Eastern Yar') meets Bembridge Harbour. The piers which once carried the Bembridge to Brading railway over the river can be seen immediately alongside the bridge. At the road junction ahead (beyond an estate of 3-storey flats) turn hair-pin right into Latimer Road. When this turns left you should proceed forward towards the Bembridge Angling Club premises and join a drive on the left alongside the harbour. When the drive soon divides into two take the right-hand branch; the harbour with its landing stages will then be on your right and a stone wall on your left.

The house behind the wall occupies the site of St. Helen's Tide Mill. A large mill-shaft rests above the entrance gate and can be seen from that other branch of the drive. Where the stone wall comes to an end turn left and walk the short distance (15-20 paces) to the boundary of the old mill pond (now a tidal marsh). Turn right here and go along the boundary wall, with the stone wall of a boat house on your right. You will soon be steered left on to a long, straight mill-dam starting from the end of the boathouse. Looking back you will have a good view of the tide-mill portal where seawater entered the mill from the mill-pond. Seawater was collected in the pond on an incoming tide by means of sluice gates. The gates would then be closed and the stored water used to drive the mill.

Keep straight on from the end of the mill-dam and cross the Duver in the direction of a red-roofed house standing behind conifers. You will soon meet a drive and a National Trust car park. **(12)** This is where we meet up with those who crossed the harbour by ferry.

The Duver was given to the National Trust in 1961 by the Royal Isle of Wight Golf Club. It is designated a Site of Special Scientific Interest, chiefly on account of its population of wild plants. It is the only location on the Island of the rare autumn squill scilla autumnalis, which flowers in August and September. Other plants to look out for are the tree lupin, sea buckthorn, sea holly; sea bindweed, evening primrose, sea heath — a small sample of the 250 or so species that are known to grow here.

Those who crossed the Duver by ferry will have missed seeing the Tide-mill House and the tidal pond and dam. To make amends go inland from the car park (perpendicular to the drive) proceed across the Duver to a National Trust plinth. The Tide-Mill House is near the far end of the dam (see page 48). See you back here later!

Before continuing the walk, railway enthusiasts should inspect the old carriages on the Duver shore seaward of the car park. These were originally in service on London's Metropolitan Railway. From the car park go forward along the drive; you will pass a large red-roofed house on the right and the Old Golf Clubhouse on the left. The clubhouse is used by the National Trust as 'self-catering' holiday accommodation.

St. Helens Sea-Mark Church

Where the drive turns left just beyond a stone cottage you will find a stile leading forward into a field; but before going over that stile a few paces along the track on the right will take you into a pleasant grassy area with a close-up view of the old Sea-mark Church tower. Although the tower dates back to the thirteenth-century there was a small Cluniac priory here well before that — from about 1090 A.D. In the sixteenth-century the church was reported to be in a bad state; and in 1720 the sea dealt a mortal blow from which the building never recovered. Only the tower remained; this was faced with brick and painted white for use as a sea-mark.

Now go over that stile and along the right-hand edge of a field, passing under low-voltage pylons. At the far right-hand corner of the field go over a stile on the right and into another field. Cross a stream almost immediately, go forward about 15 yards, turn left, then strike across the field to a kissing-gate beside a wooden pylon at the top right-hand corner. Turn right in the lane here and go along this to meet the entrance drive to Priory Hotel just before a right-hand turn. Go along the hotel drive (yes it *is* a right of way) to a pair of white gate-posts close to a large oak tree. Leave the drive here by going half-left along a good path under trees, with a wood on the right and a field on the left. The path terminates just beyond a cottage terrace on the right (the wood also terminates here, and a footpath comes in from the left — at a stile). Turn right into a rough drive and stay in this as it runs straight and true for ½ mile or so.

When you are within a stone's-throw of the sea at Seagrove Bay turn left into a footpath immediately beyond the public toilets (useful reference points these!). The path passes between houses and soon joins a rough drive. Stay in the drive when it curves left and uphill beyond the houses. Unless cleared away by the time of your arrival the rubble along the shore is all that remains of Seaview's 1,050-foot pier. Built on the suspension principle this fine piece of engineering was a great tourist attraction as well as being a stopping-off point for steamers from Portsmouth. The pier started life in 1880 and was derelict by the 1940's. Severely damaged by a storm in 1951 it became a hazard and was subsequently dismantled.

Stay in the road until you come to the shops and the crossing with High Street. Turn right into High Street and follow this down to the sea and Nettlestone Point. You may be fortunate to have synchronised your arrival here with one of Seaview's colourful yachting events; and this, together with tea and home-made cakes at the Old Fort Cafe, will make for a memorable visit.

Turn right just beyond the yacht club and proceed along the sea wall. (If the sea is lashing the wall you could take the alternative route along

Bluett Avenue). You will soon meet the seaward end of Salterns Road at a tollgate. Salterns Road has a row of fine old cottages once occupied by Seaview's saltworkers. Salt was a thriving industry here in the early 1800's. The evaporating ponds (salterns) in which sea-water was collected were situated on land behind the cottages. After evaporation the resulting brine solution was boiled in special pans until salt crystals precipitated. Continue along the sea wall with the toll road (Duver Road) running parallel on your left. At the next tollgate ahead go straight on along the coast road until it turns left at The Battery Hotel. A few paces forward and Puckpool Park Mortar Battery, with its ditch and ramparts will be on your left.

Even if the military goings-on of our Victorian ancestors do not excite your imagination, you have nothing to lose by walking through Puckpool Park (which is quite pleasant and includes a cafeteria) and rejoining the sea wall further along. Access to the park is either through a gate where the road turns left or by a footbridge linking the sea wall to the rampart. The battery is extremely important historically because it is the

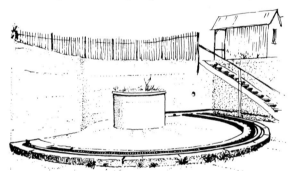

Armstrong Barbette Mounting, Puckpool Park

only place in England where the Armstrong Barbette gun mounting can be seen in situ. The mounting is at the southern end of the battery and can be identified from its large cylindrical pivot block and toothed metal arc. Puckpool's mortar shells were considered to be effective against the battleships of the day since they could be directed at the relatively thin upper decks rather than the thick, less penetrable, hulls. Aiming was difficult, of course, and a 'hit' less likely than with conventional line-of-site artillary. During World War II the battery became H.M.S. Medina, with light anti-aircraft guns installed on the old emplacements.

The next landmark along the sea wall is the castellated Appley Tower. This is on the fringe of the one-time Appley Hall Estate, now Appley Park — a public open space. The Hall itself was demolished in the 1960's to make way for a housing estate.

The wall on your left as you pass the Inshore Lifeboat Station encloses the grounds of St. Cecilia's Abbey, where the Ryde Sisters lead the contemplative life of the Benedictine Order. Although much of their time is taken up with intercession and praise, Bible study and song, theirs is not a passive existence. Weaving, bookbinding, translation, calligraphy, poultry farming and horticulture are some of the practical activities of this industrious community. They are also widely known for their recordings of Gregorian Chants, which have brought them world-wide acclaim. You may catch a glimpse of the Abbey Chapel as you walk alongside the boating lake; also Appley House close by. The House was built in the 1720's by the notorious smuggler Daniel Boyce. The cellars in which contraband was kept is now used by the Sisters for the storage of altar bread, a home-baked product 'exported' to churches throughout the country.

The Boating Lake is next to appear — and Ryde Esplanade. A memorial tablet in Ashley Gardens on the south side of the esplanade (opposite Peter Pan's playground) remembers the tragic drowning of more than 1000 officers and men of the Royal George, which sank in Spithead in 1782. Hundreds of bodies were washed up in nearby Dover Street and lie buried beneath the seafront.

"Toll for the Brave!
The Brave that are no more!
All sunk beneath the wave
Fast by their native shore!

Apparently it was all due to 'Admiralty incompetence' —

It was not in the battle;
No tempest gave the shock;
She sprang no fatal leak,
She ran upon no rock."   (William Cowper 1783)

The ex-London Underground trains disappearing under the Esplanade are running on a section originally opened in 1880 (in spite of '1881' on the tunnel entrance). This extended the established Ventnor to Ryde (St. John's Road) service to Ryde Esplanade and Ryde Pier Head. I have the great satisfaction of being able to recall many steam-hauled journeys along this line in the 1950's when I travelled between my home and R.A.F. Ventnor.

If your legs will carry you uphill in Union Street (opposite Ryde Pier) you will be rewarded with the pleasing sight of the Royal Victoria Arcade; and with further exertion you can view the fine Town Hall in Lind Street with its attractive clock tower. Ryde came into its own after the commencement of a regular ferry service from the mainland in 1826; and Queen Victoria's arrival on the Island added a fashionable turn to the town's development. It became popular to mimic the Queen's Island home, Osbourne House — on a smaller scale of course.

Bembridge Ferry Crossing

With your back to the memorial fountain and the entrance to The Point car-park on your right, go forward across the left-hand shore of the sand-dune with your sights aimed at a red and white striped pole (and a warning notice for bathers) at the mouth of the harbour, where hopefully your ferryman will be waiting. A variation on this is to go into the car-park itself and vere left towards the striped pole. The ferry will put you down in front of Attrill's boatyard (more-or-less). I have seen wooden scale models of new battleship designs in the water here, looking for all the world like large toys.

On leaving the shore go between the two large houses and forward across the Duver to a National Trust car park just to the right of a drive. Now back to (12) on page 49.

Returning to Bembridge

Bus route 8/8A.
Seaview Services run an hourly bus service between Seaview and Ryde, via Puckpool Park.

Accommodation

Wookey Guest House, George Street, Ryde. Tel. (0983) 64202.
Holmleigh Guest House, Castle Street, Ryde. Tel. (0983) 62278.
The Vine Guest House, 16 Castle Street, Ryde. Tel. (0983) 66633.
Montague House, 37 Dover Street, Ryde. Tel. (0983) 611312.
Georgian Hotel, George Street, Ryde. Tel. (0983) 63989.
Merrywood, 48 St. Thomas Street, Ryde. Tel. (0983) 64526.

Refreshments available at Bembridge, St. Helen's Duver, Seaview, Puckpool Park and Ryde.

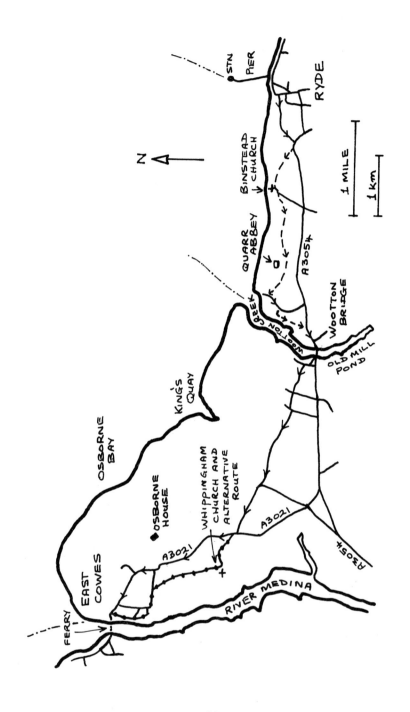

STN PIER

RYDE

N

1 MILE

1 km

BINSTEAD CHURCH

QUARR ABBEY

A3054

WOOTTON BRIDGE

WOOTTON CREEK

OLD MILL POND

KING'S QUAY

OSBORNE BAY

OSBORNE HOUSE

WHIPPINGHAM CHURCH AND ALTERNATIVE ROUTE

A3021

A3021

A3054

EAST COWES

RIVER MEDINA

FERRY

54

8. RYDE TO EAST COWES

DISTANCES: Wootton Bridge 3.5 miles (5.6km)
East Cowes 7.5 miles (12.1km)

CAR PARKING at Ryde: (1) Plenty of Sea Front parking, but this is expensive.
(2) Two car parks in St. Thomas Street, near Western Esplanade.
(3) Roadside parking in East Hill Road — near the Boating Lake, and free!

There are mixed feelings about this part of the Coast Path. None of it lies along the coast, and the second half — from Wootton to Cowes — is almost entirely road! The good news is that the first half — from Ryde to Wootton — includes the delightful district of Binstead and Quarr. And there's a ray of hope for the future: the Department of the Environment has been under pressure to allow public access to the coastline along the periphery of the Osborne Estate(the grounds of Queen Victoria's Island home). This would eliminate much of the road walking and greatly improve the quality of the coast path. But until that comes about there are a few options open to you. From Wootton Bridge you could return to Ryde or go forward to Cowes by bus (route 4). If you are car-based you could drive to the far end of Spencer Road, Ryde (NB: no access from the A3054); park your car; walk to Binstead and Quarr; then return to your car by the same route. Last but not least you could simply walk those four road-miles from Wootton Bridge.

The Prince Consort, Ryde

With the Ryde bus terminus and the pier entrance on your right walk along the Esplanade to where the road doubles back in a loop. Then go forward from the loop into St. Thomas Street. The Prince Consort — on the right in St. Thomas Street — was formerly the Royal Victoria Yacht Club, which in its day helped to make Ryde a fashionable holiday resort. It's an imposing building from the seaward side, but you may find it boarded-up and neglected.

Walk uphill in St. Thomas Street to the first turning on the right — Buckingham Road. When the road meets a cul-de-sac and turns left (still Buckingham Road) — go uphill to its junction with Spencer Road. Turn right into Spencer Road and stay in this to its end. The final part is roughly surfaced and terminates at a kissing-gate without linking-up with the main road (A3054). Turn half-right from the kissing-gate and join the tarmac path (Ladies Walk) signposted to Binstead and Quarr — a fine path for cycling were it not prohibited!

Binstead Church

Now it's a long, straight stretch all the way to Binstead Church: firstly between Ryde Golf Club links; then downhill to cross a stone bridge over a stream; finally uphill to the church. And what a lovely corner this is, with a well-placed churchyard seat on which to rest your tiring limbs! There is an apparent unity about the church, even though the chancel is early Norman (or thereabouts) and the nave 1844! The new nave roof owes its presence to a disastrous fire that occurred in 1969. A short distance from the east end of the church a gravestone relates the sad death of Thomas Sivell 'cruelly shot' by customs men in 1785. He was mistaken for a smuggler while going about his honest work as a Solent ferryman. Nearer our own time is the legend of a World War I pilot who crashed nearby. His ghost still haunts these parts apparently.

With the church on your right turn left into a tarmac drive and, after about 100 yards, right (opposite 'Crossways') into Church Road. Follow the left-hand curve of Church Road as far as a house called 'Little Fold' — just before a line of new houses on the left. Turn right into the bridleway directly opposite 'Little Fold'; this is signposted to Quarr and Fishbourne. Ignore the right-hand branching footpath almost immediately (this is a short path leading to the coast) and go forward in the bridleway under trees. At an imposing entrance gate ahead a path goes half-left along the edge of a wood. At this corner of the wood — on your left, and not far beyond the wire fence — can be seen some of the overgrown pits of the old Binstead stone quarries. These quarries are famous for having provided quality limestone for some of the finest buildings in the land, including Winchester and Chichester Cathedrals. The best of the stone was worked out as long ago as the fourteenth-century although production of an inferior grade continued right up until 1850.

The path along the edge of the wood eventually meets a road — beside a house called 'Boulders Mead'. Turn right here and stay in this tree-lined road until you are confronted by an iron gate not far beyond an estate of large houses. The gate leads you on to a wide, rough drive and out into the open.

Very soon you will see the ruins of the ancient 'Abbey of Our Lady of the Quarry' (or more commonly 'Quarr Abbey'), a monastery founded in the year 1132 and constructed with local Binstead limestone. So successful was this community that it was soon able to establish monasteries elsewhere. Concern has been expressed about the state of repair of the ruins. I must confess I like it the way it is, because for me the contemplation of history is at its best where the relics of Man's past have been left to the will of nature. (A short-sighted attitude perhaps, and not exactly in the interests of future generations!). The large barn attached to an old cottage (Old Abbey Farm) was the storehouse of the monastery. As you pass this way it is salutary to note that more-or-less beneath your feet — where the Abbey church once stood — lie the mortal remains of Baldwin de Redvers, Earl of Devon and founder of the monastery, and those of a bishop and a princess! The stone trough in the front garden of the cottage is one of two removed from the site of the church in 1856. The remains of notable persons and benefactors were placed in these following exhumation.

Continuing forward and passing Quarr Abbey Lodge on your right you will have sight of the 'new' Abbey just topping the trees ahead. When you reach those trees you will be met by the Abbey drive. Visitors are welcome to view the Abbey church and attend its services; and purchases may be made from a small bookshop. If you chance to meet any of the monks you will find them most friendly and courteous. All in all a delightful and worthwhile diversion.

Back on the wide rough track the Abbey gardens will be on your right as you go uphill. You will then pass another Abbey drive and a house called 'Mary Mead' before you descend the hill to an iron gate. Continue straight on down to meet a road directly opposite the Fishbourne Inn. Turn left here (or right, for an excellent view from Wootton Creek) and go along the road, passing Fishbourne ferry terminal on your right. This may be your first opportunity to see one of the new Sealink car ferries at close hand.

Car ferry

Continue along the road to a telephone box on the right (the road curves left here) and join a footpath signposted to Kite Hill. This narrow path leads you down to a tree-lined lane where you should turn left. When the lane eventually turns hairpin-left go straight on into a wood ahead — ignoring a track going off right immediately and one going left to a timber house about 50 yards further on. The woodland path falls and rises and joins a tarmac drive with houses on the left. When the drive meets the A3054 road turn right and go downhill to Wootton Bridge.

The large expanse of water south of the bridge was once the tidal pond for Wootton Mill. The mill depended for its operation on the storage in the pond of both fresh and tidal water. It was built a very long time ago, and was managed by the monks from Quarr Abbey. The mill's outfall can still be seen behind the modern Weir Cottage on the west bank of the river. Weir Cottage stands on the site of the mill; and what is now the Sloop Inn was once the miller's house. The pond has had a measure of public attention in recent times. An application to use this for water-skiing was turned down by the Medina Planning Commitee in 1983: a victory for conservation and good-sense.

Now it's your moment of decision: bus to Cowes (or Ryde), or walk to Cowes along what is 99% road. The road is not all bad: much of it is a pleasant country way; and it provides an opportunity to visit Prince Albert's church at Whippingham (along with coachloads of tourists!) and to enjoy a distant view of the old paddle steamer 'Ryde Queen'.

If you are using an old 1-inch O.S. map you may think that the 'Coast Path' from Wootton follows a long time-consuming loop around 'Holiday Village'. I am pleased to say that this particular 'detour' — which I would not wish on anyone — has been deleted from the official route of the Coast Path. Instead we make our way between the houses to join Footways on the north-west side of Wootton — much more direct!

Now you should position yourself immediately outside (outside!) the Sloop Inn, with the mill pond and the main road on your left. Go forward along a short rough track towards Unity Hall, passing a St. John's Ambulance H.Q. on your right. Then go along the path between the hall and a private garden; this will place you on New Road. Turn right here and walk the short distance to the Youth Centre on the left. The large playground betrays the Centre's former existance as a school. During the six weeks from mid-July until the end of August it functions as a temporary Youth Hostel. While it doesn't present the ultimate in luxury and convenience it has the distinct advantage of being easy on the pocket.

Leave New Road and walk the rough drive alongside the Youth Centre. Ignore the other rough drive behind the Centre and continue straight on to a house called Oakcroft. Go half-right here into a narrow path and follow this uphill between fences and bungalows. Turn right immediately beyond some private garages. This soon leads you on to a road (St. Edmund's Walk). Turn left and go up St. Edmund's Walk (ignoring the first turning on the right) to where it curves right. Don't go right with it but vere left between houses — to the left of house number 113. Then pass between private garages almost immediately, crossing the forecourt to a rough footpath opposite the fourth left-hand garage from the end. Follow this short path to Church Road and cross over to Footways. Go forward in Footways to a T-junction at its far end. Turn left here, then right into Brock's Copse Road after 25 yards.

Now you are almost at the start of that 'quiet country way' mentioned earlier; I hope you find it so! It takes you downhill to a bridge over Palmer's brook, then uphill to meet Alverstone Road at a junction. keep straight on here, passing the entrance to Woodhouse Farm on the right. Next to confront you (after ½ mile) is the busy A3021.

The official route now follows the A3021 to East Cowes. This is a busy road but has the virtue of being accompanied by a 'side-walk' all the way.

The alternative route is not so blessed, but includes the much-visited Whippingham Church. But for the affects of coaches plying up and down to the church, this is a quiet road and, to my mind, much to be preferred. For this reason (with apologies all round) I have appended the official route to the end of the chapter.

'Ryde Queen'

Turn right in the A3021, then first left into Beatrice Avenue; but before going forward in Beatrice Avenue look over the hedge from the grass bank south-south-west across the Medina Valley. If you possess a compass so much the better. This will give you a fix on the old paddle steamer 'Ryde Queen' berthed in a yacht harbour beside the River Medina. Alternatively look for a red funnel about one mile away! 'Ryde' went into service in 1937 on the Portsmouth to Ryde crossing and followed a distinguished career during peace and war. She was withdrawn from service in 1969 and now spends her retirement as a licensed entertainment centre (Boiler Room Discos and the like) under her new name 'Ryde Queen'.

You will pass a school on the right as you start walking along Beatrice Avenue. This hedge-lined road eventually turns left and goes downhill to meet Whippingham Church. With Whippingham on the tourist coach run you may find your walk along Beatrice Avenue potentially hazardous. So take care! The church was built in 1860 to the Prince Consort's specifications on ground previously occupied by an eleventh-century church. A sculptured stone on the outside wall of the south porch is all that's left of that early building. I wonder just how much ancient beauty was swept away! Today the church is well-adapted to the constant flow of visitors, with piped commentaries in the chancel and toilets in the cemetery.

Going right with the road (still Beatrice Avenue) you will pass a terrace of attractive alms-houses. These were built in 1880 as retirement houses for Queen Victoria's servants. The road runs parallel with the Medina Valley and passes Osborne Middle School on the right. Queen Victoria's Island home, Osborne House, is now in close range and can be visited by turning right into Crossways Road beyond the School. At the far end of this turn left into Whippingham Road. The entrance to Osborne House is on the right. Osborne is certainly worth visiting — if you can afford it! An 'all in one' ticket allows you to visit the house and grounds and the delightful Swiss Cottage where Queen Victoria's children learnt carpentry, gardening, housekeeping and cooking.

Even if Osborne is not on your itinerary you may welcome the existance of Crossways Tearoom (in Crossways Road).

Now back to Beatrice Avenue: continue in this to meet Victoria Grove (B3321) at a crossing. Turn left here and go downhill (or cut across the green on the left); then right with the road at the bottom, and first left into Minerva Road. Turn right into Clarence Road and follow this to its far end; then turn left for the Floating Bridge. The days of the 'Bridge' may well be numbered. Thoughts about its replacement by a road bridge have surfaced from time to time over many years, but without result. I hope this bit of history goes on repeating itself!

Official route along the A3021 to East Cowes

Having turned right into the A3021 stay in this main road for almost 2 miles to East Cowes. You will pass the access points to Barton Manor Vineyards, Osborne House (Queen Victoria's home), and Norris Castle — all open to the public. Having ignored roads going off left and right — including the B3321 just beyond Osborne House — you should eventually find yourself adjacent to East Cowes Fire Station. The main road divides into two just here. Go straight on to the shopping area and turn half-left into Ferry Road. The Floating Bridge is at the far end of this.

Returning to Ryde

Bus route 4 direct to Ryde or by the more circuitous 1A from West Cowes via Newport.

Accommodation

Seamist Guest House, East Cowes. Tel. (0983) 292021 (near the Floating Bridge).
Abergwaun House, 202 Park Road, Cowes. Tel. (0983) 298034.
Caledon Guest House, 59 Mill Hill Road, Cowes. Tel. (0983) 293599.
Temporary Youth Hostel, New Road, Wootton Bridge (Youth Centre). Tel. (0983) 882348. Open from mid-July until the end of August only.

Refreshments available at Ryde, Wootton Bridge (Sloop Inn), and Cowes.

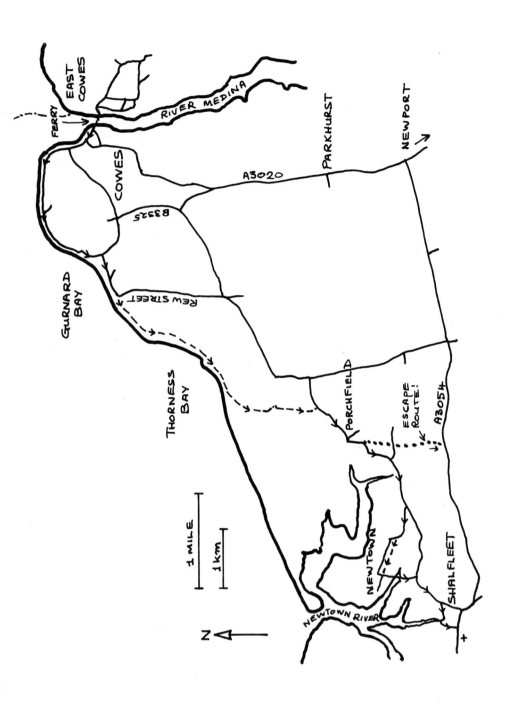

EAST COWES

FERRY

RIVER MEDINA

PARKHURST

NEWPORT

COWES

A3020

B3325

GURNARD BAY

REW STREET

THORNESS BAY

PORCHFIELD

ESCAPE ROUTE!

A3054

1 MILE

1 km

NEWTOWN

SHALFLEET

NEWTOWN RIVER

N

9. COWES TO SHALFLEET

DISTANCES: Porchfield (A3054) 6.5 miles (10.5km)
Newtown 8 miles (12.9km)
Shalfleet 9 miles (14.5km)

CAR PARKING in Cowes (1) Behind Stephen Ratsey's near the Floating Bridge (free!).
(2) At junction of Carvel Lane with Terminus Road (behind High Street).
(3) The Parade.

You may be tempted to forgo the first ¾ mile of this penultimate walk — from the Floating Bridge to The Parade (esplanade) — but in so doing you will be deprived of a walk into history. This part of Cowes is associated with some outstanding achievements in aeronautics and shipbuilding: from early sail, seaplane and submarine development to the specialised yachts, lifeboats and hovercraft of the present day.

The two miles from The Parade, Cowes, to Gurnard is entirely on hard ground — and that mostly esplanade; but it's worthwhile for all that follows: Gurnard Cliffs, Thorness Bay and the pleasant pastoral inland route to Porchfield. The final three miles through Newtown to Shalfleet are almost entirely on country roads. However, an escape route from Porchfield to the A3054 (and a bus stop) is given for those who resent all this tarmac. The cost is the exclusion of Newtown: an unforgiveable omission of a most interesting and delightful place.

As you cross the Medina on the Floating Bridge or look back from the west bank to the east, you will have a good view of two historically important buildings. The first is the Gridiron Shed situated on the seaward side of the East Cowes Floating Bridge terminus and presently owned by Clare Lallow. It is here that the famous firm of J. S. White built and launched their first seaplane. This was in 1913, in time for World War I. Further seaward the enormous dual hanger is the present home of the British Hovercraft Corporation. This is where the first successful hovercraft — the SRN I — made its proud appearance on 30th May 1959. While I applaud the progress that this British firm has made in becoming the world's largest manufacturer of hovercraft I doubt that the exchange of speed for noise is acceptable to everyone. Saunders Roe acquired the site in 1935 and constructed the flying boats that have secured the company a place in history. Their greatest work was the 140 ton Princess flying-boat; built in 1952 she was also their greatest flop.

Moving on from the ferry along Medina Road the newest industrial premises on the left are those of Stephen Ratsey, renowned for the manufacture of sails and sailcloth. When Medina Road bends left to become Mill Hill Road you should normally turn right into Birmingham Road, but a few paces uphill in Mill Hill Road will place you outside the showrooms of Carisbrooke Shipping Ltd. Not very exciting on the face of it! However, this company occupies the premises of the former Bannister Rope Works which existed here from about 1820. Rope*walks* were an essential part of rope*works* and for this reason such premises often extended over long distances — in this case 1000 feet. It is unfortunate that no-one grasped the opportunity (provided by previous owners) to preserve some of the machinery from this plant when part of the premises was converted into showrooms.

From the start of Birmingham Road you have a more-or-less direct route to the esplanade (The Parade, to be more precise). Birmingham Road connects to Shooters Hill, and Shooters Hill to High Street. On the left you will find Pascall Atkey's shop. Atkey's have been here since 1799 and are one of Britain's oldest yacht chandlers and fitters. Continue along High Street to the point where it bears left to become Bath Road. Turn right here into Watch-House Lane and go down to the Parade.

Proceeding along The Parade you will notice that the balustrade forms a semicircular bay at one point. Early photographs show an elegant Victorian brass band seated there! Another semicircular feature — the large shelter facing The Parade — has a plaque commemorating the Polish destroyer Blyskawica ('Lightning') which assisted in the defence of the town on the dreadful night of 4th/5th May 1942. By a stroke of luck Blyskawica was in Cowes for a refit — and fully armed — at the time of the Island's heaviest air-raid. It is very satisfying to know that she still exists — as a floating museum in Poland.

Before the war The Parade was graced by a fine Georgian terrace where the unattractive Osborne Court now stands. The foundations of the terrace were under suspicion and demolition unavoidable — apparently! Just beyond The Parade the exclusive Royal Yacht Squadron H.Q. looks proudly across the Solent. Its relatively modern tower stands on one of Henry VIII's 'blockhouses', defensive platforms designed specifically for the use of cannon. In its time the blockhouse has served as a prison and as a residence of the Governor of the Island (not at the same time!). Today its peak of activity occurs during Cowes Week (the first week of August) when the town is the Mecca of the yachting fraternity.

From The Parade go round the seaward side of the Royal Yacht Squadron H.Q. to the esplanade beyond. If the sea is high or turbulent, and you are in danger of getting your feet wet, you should go along the left-hand side of the H.Q. and turn first right for the esplanade. Now you have a whole mile of esplanade ahead of you; the first half takes you as far as Egypt Point, where there is a small roundabout; the second half to the start of Gurnard Bay where the road curves inland and becomes Shore Road. Don't follow this inland but continue straight on along the sea wall to a slipway. Go left in the road here and uphill to meet Shore Road again, then half-right into a tarmac path; this soon rejoins the road. Go left with the road and first right into Solent View Road. You now have ½ mile of road to take you to Gurnard Bridge; half of it is Solent View Road, the other half Marsh Road.

Having crossed Gurnard Bridge turn right immediately into a track. Marsh Road (for your information only) turns inland here and becomes Rew Street. Rew Street originally extended further northwards but has been nibbled away by the sea. It is thought that it may have terminated at a pier or landing-stage of some sort enabling communication with the mainland. Another feature long since lost to the sea is the site of the Gurnard Roman Villa. This stood beside Rew Street and was excavated in the 1860's. Roman coins and other objects have been found on the beach from time-to-time; so, if this is your lucky day . . .

The short track that you are now on has chalets on the left and a small creek with moorings on the right (if it hasn't, you're in the wrong place!). It ends at Marsh Cottage which overlooks the Solent. Go over the stile just to the left of the cottage and proceed along the low cliff edge of Gurnard Bay. The path soon crosses the seaward end of a line of chalets; then it's a clear, uneventful walk for about ⅓ mile (assuming no recent subsidence) until you reach a short stretch running under tall overhanging scrub. This terminates at a stile on the left leading into a field. Once over the stile, turn right and follow the field's right-hand edge uphill to a stile in the far right-hand corner, and continue forward with a wire fence on your left.

A variety of derelict structures makes an appearance on the right; and a group of these confronts you directly ahead (also chalets half-left). Unfortunately a large chunk of ground hereabouts has slipped seaward taking the path with it. So unless some rerouting is done before your arrival you are going to find the next few hundred yards difficult to say the least. If you keep to the top of the 'cliff' as you make your way downhill (keeping to the right of any wire fence if at all possible) you should arrive at what seems to be a relatively stable stretch of footpath. This is entered from a stile and runs along the seaward edge of a field. A second stile leads to the seaward edge of another field (wire fence left), the far side of which is lined with chalets. Now you are home and dry — I trust.

It's just about here that 'SOLO' came ashore during World War II. This was part of the PLUTO scheme (Pipeline Under The Ocean) in which fuel was pumped to the invasion forces across the Channel. These 'solo' pipes were laid under the Solent and can still be seen at low tide — seaward of a brick framework embedded in the sand.

You should soon be down at a concrete bridge positioned more-or-less on the shore. Cross this (to seaward), turn left immediately, and go along the sand dune towards a large chequered triangle. There's another triangle placed inland and a further pair out-of-sight along the coast. Together these four markers provide a 'measured mile' for shipping. During the Second World War they were used by the Navy for the calibration of ships' compasses. Vessels could often be seen lining-up with the precise angle provided by one pair of markers.

Cross the metal footbridge and go forward to a picnic area; turn half-left here into a rough uphill drive leading to Thorness Bay Holiday Centre. Passing a play area on the left and a shop on the right go up to a Y-junction in the drive where the permanent chalets start. Take the left-hand branch (No-through road sign) and walk uphill, keeping to the main drive (the widest) until you are within arm's reach of the entrance gate. Turn right and, with a hedge on your left, go forward for 100 yards to a gap on the left. Cross a footbridge here, and then a stile. The stile will usher you into a long, narrow field. An opening at the far end of the field will lead you out on to a drive.

Turning left in the drive you will soon pass chalets on the left and farm buildings on the right. Just beyond the farm buildings, and directly opposite the holiday centre's H.Q., turn right to a stile, signposted 'Porchfield'. Those farm buildings will now be on your right; when you are level with the 'end' of them (if you see what I mean!) go through a gap in the hedge ahead, turn left and walk downhill — with the hedge on your left. Cross the stile in the far left-hand corner of the field and continue straight on — with a hedge still on your left — to a rail beside a metal gate; then on along the left-hand edge of another field to an exit in its far left-hand corner; then yet another field (with a wood on the left) to join a road at its far left-hand corner.

Turn right in the road and walk down to Porchfield, where you will have the welcome sight of a shop and a pub. Go beyond these to the War Memorial and the Village Hall and follow the road as it curves left on its way to Shalfleet. You now have about three miles of pavement-less road relieved by Newtown at the half-way point. If this is beyond your limits of tolerance you could take advantage of the 'escape route' mentioned earlier. This starts at the next right-hand bend in the road and runs across fields for one mile to the A3054 where a bus stop is the guarantee of your return to West Cowes — eventually. Directions are given at the end of this chapter.

If you have elected to stay the course to Shalfleet you will meet the next road-junction at about half-a-mile from Porchfield. Keep right here (for Newtown) and continue to the next junction half-a-mile or so ahead. Go half-right along the road signposted to Newtown. You will find Vicarage Lane along this road on the left. Don't go down there but do take note of the National Trust information board referring to the site of Newtown's Old Vicarage Ground. This is a wild and beautiful wood with fine examples of trees and shrubs planted many years ago. The vicarage itself was dismantled at the turn of the century; much of the brick and timber-work was used in the construction of a house called 'The Firs' in Undercliff Drive, St. Lawrence — on the south coast of the Island.

Continue along the road for about 250 yards from Old Vicarage lane to a stile on the left, where a signpost is aimed at Newtown. The numbered white post is one of the stations of Newtown's Nature Trail, and our gateway into the fascinating world of an ancient borough. It is now an area of small fields and green pathways, where flowers and butterflies are given the protection that is their due; of creek and marsh where birds are esteemed for their beauty and majesty. This is in striking contrast to the 1300's when Newtown was a busy and important borough with twice the 'value' of Newport. From this peak of prosperity the town lived on for a further 500 years, but in decline. It sent two members to parliament during 250 of these years; built its own Town Hall; received vessels weighing up to 500 tons into the safety of its harbour; held weekly markets and annual fairs. The Town Hall is still there to remind us of those days, as is the quay. Less tangible are the names: Gold Street, Silver Street, Broad Street, High Street; some of them now wide green ways — ghosts of an age that is past. Newtown, together with 14 miles of estuary and coastline, is in the care of the National Trust, preserved for the benefit of present and future generations.

With all that said, you may now climb the stile! Then walk straight ahead along the left-hand side of a field and through a gap in the hedge at its far end. Continue forward and go through a narrow wood marked with a white post at its entrance. Then straight on across two fields in succession to a stile beside a large tree stump; overhead electricity wires mark the spot. Turn right almost immediately and forward again in a long, narrow field bordered by layered hedges. A ditch accompanies the field on the right; when the ditch turns right at the far end of the field go slightly right and then forward to another white post.

The small field on your right was Newtown's Bowling Green; and the ground under your feet may well be the site of a market place. With the white post and the 'Bowling Green' on your right go forward along a hedge-lined 'street' to a stile. The Map of the Borough of Newtown (dated 1768) calls this 'High Street', but to townspeople it was probably 'Silver Street'. Walk along this to a road (Broad Street) where a left turn will take you alongside a stone-built house called Noah's Ark. This was formerly an inn, and is almost certainly the oldest building in Newtown. The painted board over the door is the former inn sign, reproduced from the borough seal.

Old Town Hall, Newtown

A little further along Broad Street the Town Hall stands tall and proud, a reminder of the borough's former eminence. It served its proper function as a town hall from the time of its construction in about 1700 until its redundancy in the 1830's. Thereafter it performed variously as school, private house, youth hostel and civil defence quarters. In 1933 it was rescued from a ruinous state and presented to the National Trust by a group of anonymous benefactors who called themselves The Ferguson Gang.

Unless you walk from here to the estuary and the quay (and back) you will have done Newtown an injustice. This spur will lengthen your walk by just one mile, but the reward is well-worth the extra effort. If you intend to reserve the pleasure for another day you should read on from **(13)** on page 70 at the point where we move off from the Town Hall in the direction of Cassey Bridge.

If you are estuary-bound you should 'about turn' and go past Noah's Ark (on your right) and straight on until you arrive at the right-hand bend in the road. Turn left here and walk along Gold Street (a long narrow field) to a stile and gate leading on to a road at the far end. Go forward in the road a few paces and turn right through a gate marked March Farm House; then along a drive that soon evolves into a path running between hedges. After going through a wooden gate and passing an observation post on the right, turn left into a gravel path which runs between a field and fence on the left and marshland on the right. At the end of this turn right and cross the marsh on a long wooden footbridge. And there you have Newtown Quay — a shadow of its former glory as the Island's most important port.

The path that you are now on continues forward along a sea wall that encompasses the large area of marsh on your right. This would make a fine circular walk but for the breaches in the wall. On the night of 26th/27th November 1954 a heavy storm broke through the sea wall and inundated 130 acres of reclaimed grazing land. It has remained a marsh ever since.

The New Inn, Shalfleet

The large, square 'ponds' close to the black timber hut are reminders of the salt industry that existed here for many centuries. Sea water was collected in these shallow ponds and allowed to evaporate under the influence of sun and wind. It was then pumped into large iron pans until the salt crystallized.

Doubtless you will remember your way back to the Town Hall; if not, simply read the directions in reverse.

(13) With the Town Hall on your left go forward along Broad Street to Cassey Bridge, where Causeway Lake (one of Newtown estuary's many creeks) makes an attractive picture. Turn right at the T-junction ahead and go along this for half-a-mile to the first turning on the right at a No Through Road sign. At the end of the road — just before a cottage — turn right into a path (with a wood on the left) and follow this down to a footbridge over Shalfleet's millstream. Cross the footbridge to Mill Road, passing Shalfleet Mill on the left. This was a working mill in earlier days: not a tide-mill but driven from a pond that accompanied Mill Road all the way to the village centre. When you arrive there yourself you will find the New Inn, the church and Shalfleet Manor. The Inn is acclaimed as an excellent eating-house specialising in seafood, some of which is harvested locally.

Escape route from Porchfield

At the first right-hand bend in the road after Porchfield (grid ref. 446909) go left across a grass verge to a stile in the hedge, signposted 'Calbourne'; then forward along the left-hand edge of two fields in succession, to a road. Cross the road and go forward a short distance to a stile beside a farm track; then proceed along the left-hand edge of a field to a stile in the far left-hand corner. Cross the next, long, field to an iron gate in its far right-hand corner; then alongside a ditch on the right-hand edge of another field, to a road. Turn left and there's your bus-stop!

Returning to West Cowes

Bus route 7 to Newport then 1A to West Cowes.

Accommodation

Shalfleet House — on the A3054 ⅓-mile west of Shalfleet (a very convenient starting point for the next walk. Tel. Calbourne 280.
Mrs. Hindle, Clamerkin Farm; one mile west of Newtown. Tel. Calbourne 396.
Mrs. Simmonds, Elmsworth Farm, Porchfield. Tel. (0983) 522689.

Refreshments available at Cowes, Gurnard, Porchfield (Sportsman's Rest) and Shalfleet (New Inn).

10. SHALFLEET TO YARMOUTH

DISTANCE: 7.5 miles (12.1km)

CAR PARKING at Shalfleet   Mill Road car park.

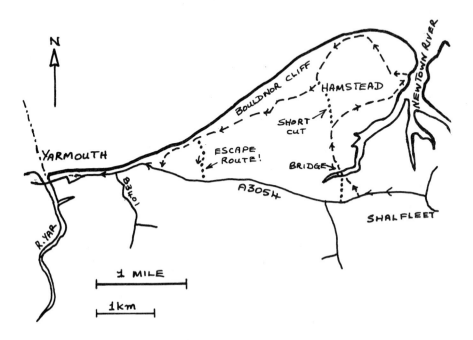

If you enjoy the quiet unmolested places this final walk will be much to your satisfaction. I doubt you will see a chalet, a caravan, a cafe or an amusement arcade along here! (although there is one small unpretentious shop at Lower Hamstead Farm serving the yachting fraternity but open to all). To add to your pleasure I can guarantee that the coast will be in view for at least one-third of the time! Part of this is estuary coast where the path clips the extremities of four of Newtown's creeks as it inscribes an anti-clockwise loop around the Hamstead peninsula. The rest is Solent coast overlooked by Hamstead and Bouldner Cliffs. At Bouldner there's a mile of crumbling cliff that can make the going variable (or difficult) and you may need to call on that inner resource of initiative and determination yet again.

With this in mind a brief visit to the church of St. Michael the Archangel would be an appropriate start to the day! The stout tower is perhaps the most outstanding feature of the church. This (the tower) was built in about 1070, only four years after the Battle of Hastings. With

71

base walls more than five feet thick, and with no direct entrance from outside, the tower became a secure refuge for the local population during sporadic French invasions. So real were these incursions that a three-pounder gun was sited at the base of the tower. The threats from without were almost matched by those from beneath: the tower had such poor foundations (ten feet of clay and water and not much else.) that serious problems arose when structural alterations were attempted. East of the church in Church Lane stands the Old Vicarage, thought to have been a pre-Reformation clergy house. It became a private house in 1871.

The walk commences with ½ mile of main road (A3054) from Shalfleet in the direction of Yarmouth. Car parking on the A3054 may prove difficult or at least hazardous — so you would do well to *walk* that short distance. But do take care.

Look for a footpath signpost half-way down the first hill beyond Shalfleet House. This is on the right-hand side of the road and points north across fields (an alternative starting point ¼ mile further along the road is detailed at the end of the chapter). From that signpost walk away from the road along the right-hand edge of a field — with a hedge on the right. On arrival at the next field you should aim at the far left-hand corner where you will find a footbridge over a narrow creek. If there's a standing crop in this field you may feel happier to walk along the field-edge.

Airborne Lifeboat

That decaying hull lying in the creek alongside the footbridge is no ordinary boat. It is, believe it or not, one of World War II's Airborne Lifeboats! Brainchild of the well-known yacht designer Uffa Fox, the Airborne Lifeboats were dropped by rescue aircraft alongside 'ditched' aircrews. The lifeboats were well-equipped to provide for long homeward journeys. A large number of them were built and they saved many lives.

The bridge will lead you on to a path, under oak trees, with the creek on your right. Fork left at a clear Y-junction in the path after 40 yards and walk the short distance (with the creek now behind you) to a forestry drive. Turn right in the drive and go down to the stone bridge over Ningwood Lake — another of Newtown Estuary's many creeks. **(14)** After passing 'Pigeon Coo' (!) Farm — an attractive tiled and white-fronted house over on your left — you will meet a Y-junction part-way up the following hill. Take the right-hand branch signposted to Lower Hamstead Farm and Creek Farm. (You could lose 1½ miles by going straight on and missing out the 'Hamstead Loop' — which would be a pity; but 'if needs must' you should go straight on, turn left with the drive at Hamstead Grange, then forward to a stile on the left just before the entrance to Woodcote Cottage. Continue from **(15)** on page 74.)

The uphill right-hand branch eventually breaks out into the open to give a fine view of the Solent and parts of Newtown Estuary. You should ignore a footpath on the left just before Creek Farm and continue ahead to Lower Hamstead Farm and 'Quay Stores'. Go over the stile here (beside an iron gate marked 'Private') and straight on to Hamstead Quay — a fine place to relax and absorb the beauty of Newtown Estuary. The estuary is a 'treasure house' for those interested in natural history. Botanically it has five distinct areas: shingle, sand, saltmarsh, woodland and pasture, accommodating more than 200 species of plants. Birds are well represented, with a species count of about 170. Palaeontologists are keenly interested in the area also, and over the years have found hundreds of fossil bones, including those of hippopotamus and elephant!

Now you should about face and go back 40 yards to a stile on the right leading into a pasture (this stile was on your left as you approached the quay). Follow the right-hand edge of the pasture (wire fence left) to a stile in its far right-hand corner; then go between marshland on the right (beyond a wire fence) and a small oak copse on the left, to a stile. You now have a total of four plank 'bridges' and two stiles to take you around the extremities of the marsh and over to its far right-hand corner. Turn right immediately after the second stile and go round the right-hand side of an oak-copse and up along the left-hand edge of a field with a hedge on the left. Go over a stile about 200 yards before the far end of the hedge and into another field. Strike half-right across this field to a stile in its far right-hand corner; then along a fine new footbridge across the head of the creek. This leads you on to the right-hand edge of a large field. Follow this field-edge to a stile at the far right-hand corner, where a flight of steps leads down to the beach.

Turn left and go along the grass verge bordering the beach. The small stone cross tucked into the trees on the left is inscribed to the memory of two young men who were 'lost at sea' in the 1930's. The grass verge soon joins a track running parallel to the coast. The large concrete ramp on the beach just here was a World War II tank landing-stage. It's not difficult to imagine the intense activity of those days! The track works its way inland from here — with fields on the left and trees on the right. At the second stile and gate ahead (after a long, steady climb) go straight on, passing a farm on the left. The track soon turns left, then right, then left again. Go up to a stile on the right just beyond the final bend — after passing the entrance drive to Woodcote Cottage. (15) Those who took the shortcut from Nunny's Wood will find the stile on their left.

Go over the stile and strike across the field to another stile under an oak tree on the far side. Continue forward across the next field to a gap in its far left-hand corner, and on again along the left-hand side of another field with a hedge on the left. After going over a stile and passing under electricity wires, cross the entrance drive to a house on the right and continue ahead to a stile under conifer trees. After passing another house on the right go ahead to a crossing drive, in which turn left (not straight on — as some maps indicate). Go along the drive for a few hundred yards; and just before this curves left turn right into a drive alongside a house called Lyndale. At the far end of this drive go left over a stile and into a narrow path. Turn right at the next stile and, after passing a house and garden on the right go ahead to another stile inside a wood. Follow the path as it cuts across the eastern end of the wood and turn half-left when you are at its far side. You should then be walking parallel to the coast, with a conifer plantation on your left and the Solent on your right. The magnificent view ahead includes Yarmouth and its pier — today's destination.

Although the directions I am giving for the reminder of the walk are based on my most recent experience you may find Nature having the last word, as pieces of the path fall victim to erosion. If you keep the coast more-or-less in sight while avoiding (where possible) the cliff edge, you should not have too much difficulty.

After about 40 yards beyond a viewpoint and seat on the right, branch half-right. A boundary stone makes its appearance on the left; keep straight on, making use of the inner path when it looks safer. You will eventually pass an old brick gun-post on the right.

The derelict stone structure a little out to sea is all that's left of a nineteenth-century pier. Bricks manufactured here at Bouldner were shipped from the pier by barge. A Medieval settlement site was excavated just a short distance from the pier (in the Yarmouth direction) in 1972 and 1975. Among the items discovered were Roman and Medieval pots, wattle hurdling, flint flakes, bones and antlers. Such finds are apparently quite common along this coast. After a few hundred yards turn right at the T-junction and left after about 10 yards; and when the path soon divides into two take the left-hand branch. This will eventually lead you down to the beach, at a small bay. If the path has fallen away and further progress has become impossible, you have no choice but to retreat — unless an alternative path has been carved through the jungle in the meantime. A suitable route for the retreat — without too much loss of face — is outlined at the end of the chapter.

About 80 yards beyond the far side of the beach you should go right at the first Y-junction, then left — almost immediately — at the second, passing a concrete building foundation on the right. Keep to the main path and, after 150 yards, turn left at a T-junction just beyond a timber footbridge. After 20 yards turn right in to a rough drive and follow this up to the A3054. A right turn here and your feet (or a bus) will take you the mile-or-so into Yarmouth.

(16) Where the road finally curves inland at 'The Common' (a picnic area) keeping right for High Street makes a pleasant entry into Yarmouth and a fine climax to the walk.

Alternative starting point

This is ¾ mile from Shalfleet at Nunney's Wood. Look for a sign-board 'Hamstead Estate', at the commencement of a wide, rough drive. Hamstead Lodge is just here; and a bus stop. Simply walk along that drive for ⅓ mile to the stone bridge across Ningwood Lake. Now back to (14) on page 73.

Retreat from Bouldner

Go back along the path until you are almost in line with the derelict pier — where the path turns right and then left after a few yards. Walk inland from this point along a clear straight path through the woods. Although not marked as a right of way this path has been used by local people for a very long time. At the far end of the path you will be confronted by buildings of one sort and another, including Bouldner Battery. Now you should make your way half-left across the complex and link up with a drive that keeps you moving in the same direction as before — south; (there is a similar drive going elsewhere — so take care!). You will soon pass a bungalow on the right; after that it's a long walk down to the A3054; then 1½ miles to Yarmouth — on foot or by bus (route 12). If you are snubbing the bus it's worth going back to **(16)** on page 75.

Returning to Shalfleet
Bus route 7.

Accommodation
Glen Lynn, Victoria Road, Yarmouth. Tel. (0983) 760698.
St. Hilda, Victoria Road, Yarmouth. Tel. (0983) 760814.
The Retreat, Cranmore. Tel. Yarmouth (0983) 760802.
Quinces, Cranmore Avenue. Tel. Yarmouth (0983) 760080 (Cranmore is 2 miles east of Yarmouth).

Refreshments available at Shalfleet (New Inn) and Yarmouth. Small shop at Lower Hamstead Farm (open mid-April — end of September).

FERRY SERVICES TO THE ISLAND

SEALINK: Lymington to Yarmouth car and passenger ferry.
                    Portsmouth to Fishbourne car and passenger
                    ferry.
                    Portsmouth to Ryde passenger ferry.

RED FUNNEL: Southampton to Cowes car and passenger ferries
                    (including a fast hydrofoil service).

HOVERTRAVEL: Southsea to Ryde passenger hovercraft.

Information about these services can be obtained from travel agents or
from the following addresses:

— Sealink Isle of Wight Services,
   P.O. Box 59, Portsmouth, PO1 2XB. Tel. (0705) 827744.

— Red Funnel Services, 12 Bugle Street, Southampton.
   Tel. (0703) 226211 (333042 outside office hours).

— Hovertravel Ltd., Clarence Pier, Southsea. Tel. (0705) 829988.

BUS SERVICES ON THE ISLAND

Southern Vectis Omnibus Company (Nelson Road, Newport, Isle of
Wight, PO30 1RD. Tel. (0983) 522456) publish separate Summer and
Winter timetables for their Island-wide service. These are a good
investment since they also include timings of Post Buses, Seaview
Services (bus from Seaview to Ryde), British Rail's service from Ryde to
Shanklin, and all the ferry services mentioned above.

TAXI SERVICES

This is a sample of the forty or so taxi firms that are in existance on the Island:

A.A.A. Taxi Service, West Wight. Tel. 761176.
Calverts Taxi Service, Totland Bay. Tel. 752413.
Chiverton's Taxis, Ventnor. Tel. 853396.
Timey's Taxis, Ventnor. Tel. 853871.
Ace Taxis, Shanklin. Tel. 866670.
Shanklin Taxi Service. Tel. 862153.
Colin's Taxi Service, Sandown. Tel. 402732.
Marktab Taxi Services, Sandown. Tel. 402012.
Bembridge Taxis. Tel. 872384.
Bill's Taxis, Nettlestone. Tel. Seaview 3157.
Como Taxis, Ryde. Tel. 63224.
Q Cars, Ryde. Tel. 62333.
Wootton Bridge 24-hour Service. Tel. 883421.
J. H. Rounsevell, East Cowes. Tel. 294624.
Russell's Taxis, Cowes. Tel. 292083.
Cookes Cars, Porchfield. Tel. 525626.

Taxi Ranks:
Cowes, Fountain Pier. Tel. 297134.
East Cowes, Trinity Road. Tel. 297024.
Ryde Esplanade. Tel. 64634.
Newport, Town Lane. Tel. 526776.